Basic Carpentry and Interior Design

Projects for the Home & Garden

Anna and Anders Jeppsson

4880 Lower Valley Road • Atglen, PA 19310

Published by Schiffer Publishing, Ltd.
4880 Lower Valley Road
Atglen, PA 19310
Phone: (610) 593-1777; Fax: (610) 593-2002
E-mail: Info@schifferbooks.com

For our complete selection of fine books on this and related subjects, please visit our website at **www.schifferbooks.com**. You may also write for a free catalog.

This book may be purchased from the publisher. Please try your bookstore first.

We are always looking for people to write books on new and related subjects. If you have an idea for a book, please contact us at **proposals@schifferbooks.com**.

Schiffer Publishing's titles are available at special discounts for bulk purchases for sales promotions or premiums. Special editions, including personalized covers, corporate imprints, and excerpts can be created in large quantities for special needs. For more information, contact the publisher.

In Europe, Schiffer books are distributed by
Bushwood Books
6 Marksbury Ave.
Kew Gardens
Surrey TW9 4JF England
Phone: 44 (0) 20 8392 8585; Fax: 44 (0) 20 8392 9876
E-mail: info@bushwoodbooks.co.uk
Website: www.bushwoodbooks.co.uk

Translation by Carol Huebscher Rhoades
Copyright © 2013 by Schiffer Publishing, Ltd.; © 2007 by Anna and Anders Jeppson and ICA Book Publishers under the title *Snickra själv till hemmet & trädgården*

Library of Congress Control Number: 2013937344

Design Adaptation by Mark David Bowyer
Type set in Myriad Pro / NewsGoth Cn BT

ISBN: 978-0-7643-4363-6
Printed in China

Preface

Many times I've wondered why we can't go into a furniture store and shop just like everyone else. Why do we always have to ask ourselves: "Couldn't we make this ourselves?" Or: "That's nice but wouldn't it work better if we changed this or that?" Or: "Why pay so much for something that you can make a lot less expensively yourself?"

If this sounds familiar, chances are you have a husband like mine — a man who thinks that, and after a day of work at the advertising agency, finds it totally relaxing to go down to the carpentry shed and build something. Yes, and, as it so often happens, one project is barely finished before the next one is underway.

The goal and the need are often mine, but I turn the construction over to Anders' capable hands. Although it is best if I keep away from the woodworking, when the piece is finished it's my turn to immortalize it.

All the projects in this book come from our home, and it has been incredibly fun — and sometimes a little challenging, it must be admitted — to present them in this way. Our goal and our hope throughout are to inspire others to make things themselves.

You can choose to follow the instructions precisely or change them so that the desired product suits a specific need. Here are a couple of pieces of advice we want to share: be careful and take your time. Don't be afraid to make mistakes. And, according to Anders, you can do it without a plane, at least to begin with.

-- Anna Jeppsson

Contents

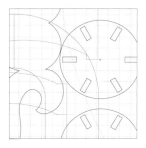

Built-in Bookcases

**It must have taken 200 feet
of lumber to make our built-in bookcases,
but it was worth every foot!**

For eight weeks, the wood lay in lofty piles on the living room floor to dry and adjust to room temperature. Friends came for dinner and we stumbled, irritated, over the pile of wood when we set the table. However, we didn't want the shelf boards to become "propeller wood" over time.

The house was built in 1932 and we wanted the shelves to look as if they had been there ever since. To achieve that goal, we used latex sealant to fill in all the gaps and spaces in between. It was especially important to have the crown molding flush with the ceiling. We used the latex filler quite a bit. It is these little details that transform new additions into "original décor."

A bus stop located just outside the living room window made it necessary to have some protection from peeping eyes, but, true to habit, we wanted an alternative to curtains. So, why not shutters – on the inside?

Built-in Bookcases

Making bookshelves with veneers would be expensive and using sheets of wood such as particle board would be totally out of character for our house. Besides, the boards would soon look like hammocks. We chose tongue-and-groove paneling, a cheaper yet strong alternative, although it required a little extra work.

Materials

Tongue and groove boards: 4/5" x 3-7/10"
(21x95mm), approx 656 ft. (200m)
Masonite: 4 sheets each 41" x 104" (1040x2650mm)
 4 pieces each 5-3/25" x 10-7/25" (130x261mm)
Decorative trim: 4/5" x 1-4/5" (21x45mm), 4 pieces
each @ 3 yds. (2,550mm)
Floor strips: 15 ft. (4.5m)
Vertical supports: ½" x ½" (15x15mm), 4 pieces each
@ 8-1/2 ft. (2600mm)
Molding: country house style ½" x 2-3/10" (15x59mm), 20ft. (6m)
Shelf supports: 4/5" x ½" (21x15mm), 24-1/2 yds. (22.5m)
Rails: 1-4/5" x 1-4/5" (45x45mm), 26 ft. (8m)

Instructions

1. Glue the tongue-and-groove sheets together in threes for the sides A, shelves B and top/base boards C and D, with the better side facing out, up (down for the "ceiling"), and to the front, respectively. Assemble so that the unattractive sides will face in, down (up), and to the back so that they won't be visible when the bookcases are finished.
2. Remove any marking or notches with a circle saw or plane (see Illustration 1).
3. Sand with a belt sander, spackle and sand once more. Don't spackle and sand too much—the shelves should still look like they are made with lumber.
4. Cover all the knots with wood filler or shellac.
5. Trim the finished sheets for the shelves, sides and supports.
6. Assemble as shown in the illustration.
7. Glue and firmly screw in all the rails for the shelves and frame. Take note of the small extra pieces that the frame is mounted to at the top and bottom. The horizontals at the top should be mounted in front of the frame and the horizontals at the bottom between the frame sections. Screw in from the front.
8. Join the frame, at the top and the bottom, into the crosspieces F [1-4/5" x 1-4/5" (45x45mm)] with screws.
9. Nail the masonite sheet (G) on the back.

10. Attach the bookcases to the wall with screws through crosspieces F. Make sure that the bookcases are spaced enough apart from each other at the corner so that there is room for the molding (see Illustration 2).
11. Assemble the shelves. Screw on the lowest one and the shelf in the center; the others can lay on their supports. The top "shelf" is not actually a shelf but, instead, it forms the inner "ceiling" and should be screwed into its supports from below.
12. Cut grooves in the decorative trim [4/5" x 1-4/5" (21x45mm)], cut them to the correct length and attach them with glue and brads on the front edge of the cases. The decorative trim extends from the floor up to the top of the frame.
13. Nail a small piece of masonite (I) at the top of the visible sides to take up the line from the rim.
14. Attach the floor strip J between the decorative trim and the visible sides.
15. Mount the crown molding K at the ceiling all around the bookcase.
16. Attach the vertical supports L against the wall on the visible sides (otherwise some of the masonite will be visible).

Finishing

There might be some gaps here and there, but latex sealant will come to the rescue. Begin by covering any knots with wood filler. Next, go over all the joins and gaps with latex sealant, sand lightly, and then paint. Primer is easier to apply and cheaper than enamel. Apply two coats of primer, sanding lightly between coats. Sand and finish with one coat of enamel.

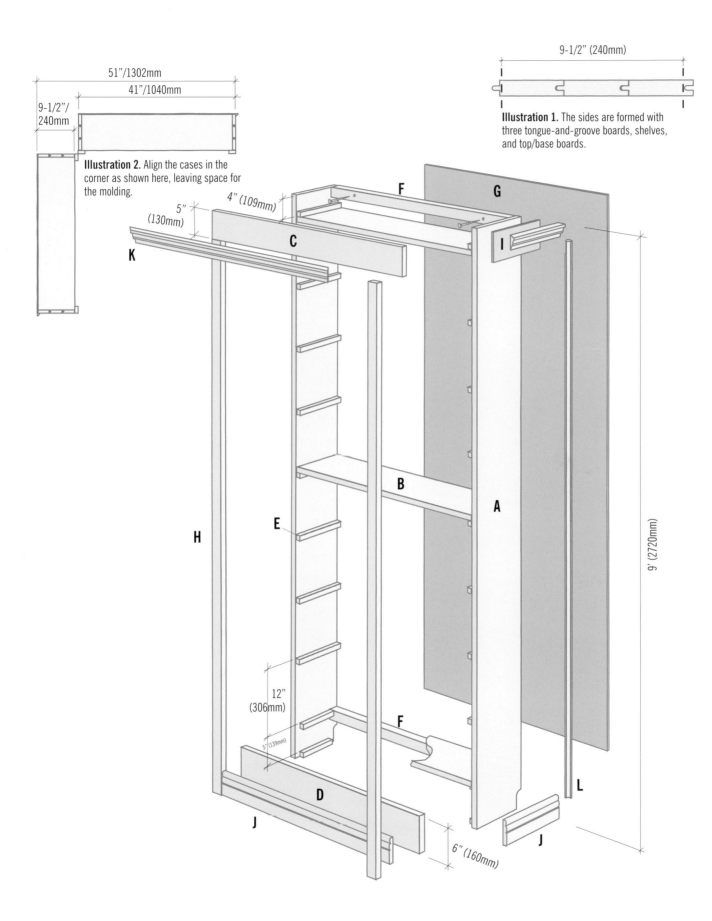

9-1/2" (240mm)

Illustration 1. The sides are formed with three tongue-and-groove boards, shelves, and top/base boards.

51"/1302mm

41"/1040mm

9-1/2"/ 240mm

Illustration 2. Align the cases in the corner as shown here, leaving space for the molding.

5" (130mm)

4" (109mm)

F

G

C

K

I

A

B

E

H

12" (306mm)

5" (139mm)

F

D

9' (2720mm)

J

6" (160mm)

J

L

9

The shutters are made from sheets of particle board and have the same striped and frosted glass as the outer door. Every morning, I open the shutters, which don't take up much room because of their accordion construction. The panels glide together and the light slips in.

Shutters

Materials

Glulam: 7/10" x 11-4/5" x 94-1/2" (18x300x2400mm), 6 sheets

Glass: 3/20" (4mm) thick, beveled, 6 pieces each 20-4/5" x 5-1/2" (530x140mm)

24 hinges: (4 for each "fold")

Instructions

1. Measure how wide and high the glulam sheets should be to fit the window. Take into consideration the thickness of the hinges.

2. Cut the glulam sheets.

3. Cut out the holes for the glass. First, 1/2" (12mm) deep from the back and then to the measurements of the glass. Next, from the front, 1/5" (7mm) deep and 1/2" (12mm) less than both the length and width of the glass, to shape a groove for the glass.

4. Set in the glass and secure each pane with a very fine batten (a "tongue" from a tongue-and-groove board works well) or with putty.

5. Mount the hinges.

Finishing

Finish the shutters as for the bookcases.

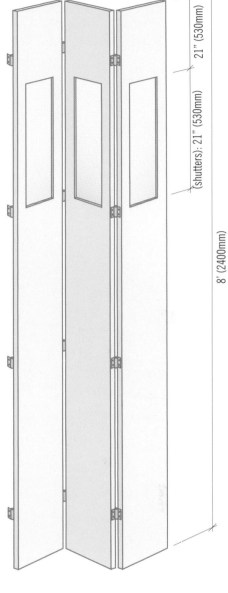

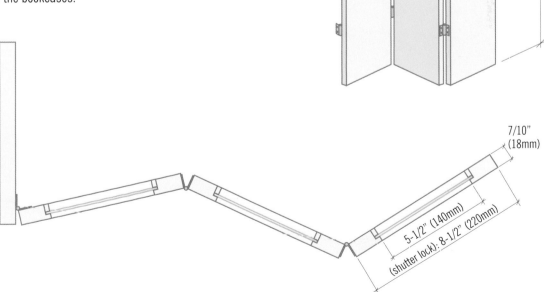

Children's Book Ends

This little bed is not just a toy. It is also a book end.
The book end will hold up a large number
of books and is, in addition, very stable.

We've had several children's book ends. They were very nice, colorful and bright, but we got tired of seeing the books fall down like dominoes. What they lacked was stability and weight.

Here are two bookends that were, of course, decorated according to the children's ideas and taste. The base is a thin wood board with the bed placed on one half and the books on the other. The books add weight to the support.

Making the bookends like little doll beds was a simple choice for us. Our children have taken cuddly toys with them to bed since they were born. Some children might prefer a car instead or maybe a bus?

A few of Hilda's many tigers look like they are very comfortable in this olive green bed, among the flowers and wild strawberries strung on a thread.

13

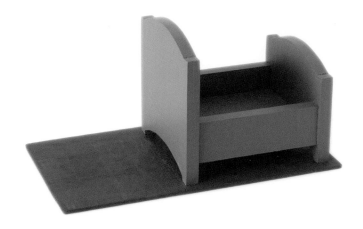

Materials

Not much is needed. Make the piece out of scrap wood, plywood, MDF (medium density board) or some boards.

3/20 (4mm) plywood for the base.
Glue
Screws
Nails

Instructions

1. Draw and then cut the pieces.

2. Glue the long sides of A to the base of the bed B as follows: Hammer small, fine nails in the long sides, nip off the nail heads, add glue and press together. The nails keep the pieces aligned. Let dry.

3. Glue on the bed ends C the same way.

4. Cut the base D.

5. Place the bed on the base and mark the placement of the legs. Bore holes for the screws and countersink.

6. Counterbore the legs, pour in a little glue and screw on the bed securely.

7. Paint and decorate with craft paints.

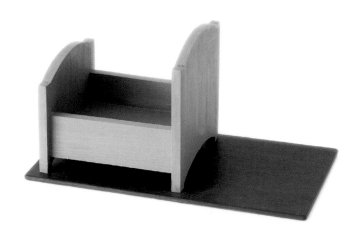

The bookend is shown in two sizes, a smaller
one (at the top) and a larger one (below).

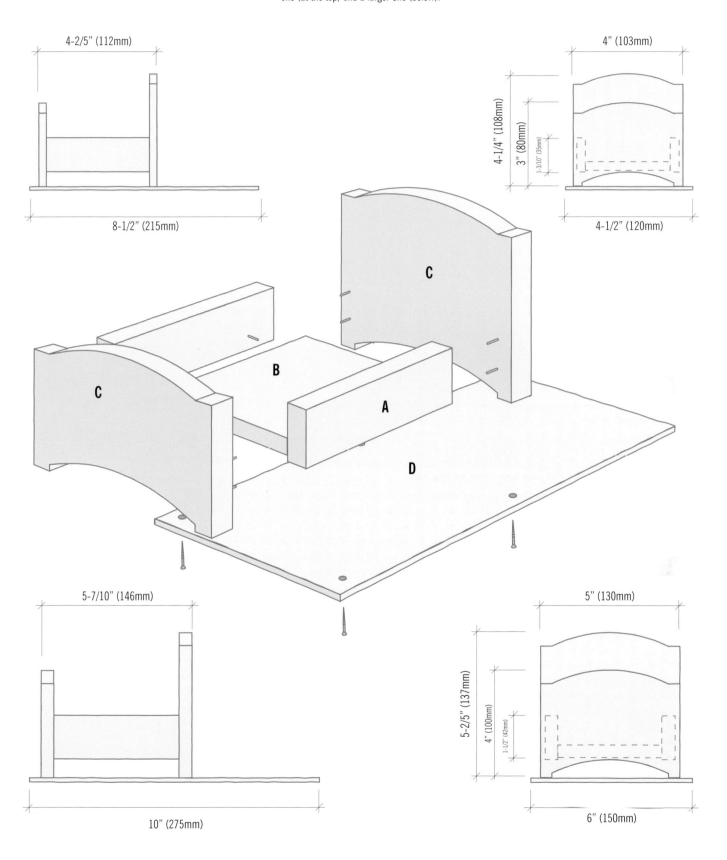

4-2/5" (112mm)

8-1/2" (215mm)

4" (103mm)

4-1/4" (108mm)

3" (80mm)

1-3/10" (35mm)

4-1/2" (120mm)

C

B

A

C

D

5-7/10" (146mm)

10" (275mm)

5" (130mm)

5-2/5" (137mm)

4" (100mm)

1-1/2" (42mm)

6" (150mm)

Radiator Cover

It's not always about having to hide it. Another, perhaps more important reason, is protection. Old radiators are hard and children are soft. Here's our solution to the problem.

Radiator covers have long been popular and, over the years, we've seen many variations.

In our house, there was an "original" made to look like a radiator cover from the 1930s, a cover that we considered both timeless and attractive. We've built several radiator covers following that design. The photo here shows the one built for the bathroom.

The cover is not only attractive, but it also functions as an extra little shelf.

Maybe we don't clean behind the radiator often enough, but, when it's time, we can simply lift off the cover.

The original radiator cover made with oak has retained its brown color and some surface nicks.

Materials

All measurements calculated to fit the radiator.

Rails: planed wood 3/5" x 9/10" (16 x 22mm)

Frame: planed wood 3/5" x 1-3/10 (16 x 34mm)

Sides and top: planed wood, glulam or MDF, dimensions determined by depth of radiator.

Glue

Wood dowel pins

Screws

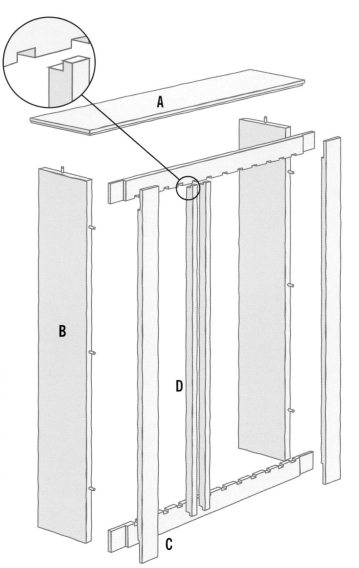

Instructions

1. Measure and cut all pieces.

2. Profile cut along the sides and front edge of board A.

3. Join sides B and board A with dowels and glue. Clamp and let dry.

4. Cut and chisel out the notches for rails D with approx 4/5" (20mm) space in between the top and bottom parts of frame C.

5. The pieces of the frame are mounted with halving joints. Cut, glue, and clamp. Let the glue dry.

6. Join frame C to the sides of B with the dowels and glue.

7. Make 3/5" (16mm) deep halving joints at the ends of slats D, using a saw and chisel (see drawing). Make sure that the rails fit firmly in the frame.

8. Glue rails D into frame C, clamp and let dry. Staple on the back between the rails and the frame.

9. Place the keyhole fitting on the back of the sides to make it easy to remove the radiator cover for cleaning.

10. Cover all the knots with wood filler. Apply two coats of primer. Sand and paint with enamel.

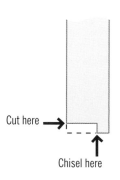

Cut here →

↑ Chisel here

Small Shelf

This shelf joins the two pieces of bench lumber into a "T" with the help of glue and dowel pins.

You can't have too many small shelves. This is a little one, a simple idea for using up the last pieces of scrap wood from the bench shelves in the kitchen. Rotating metal hooks are attached to each side – for hanging wire wisps or perhaps necklaces or even jackets depending on where the shelf is located.

Materials

Leftover pieces from a bench plank of solid wood, 1-1/10" (27mm) thick
2 dowel pins
Keyhole brackets
Hooks

Instructions

1. Cut the pieces, 6" x 15-1/2" (150x397mm) and 6" x 7-3/10" (150x185mm)

2. Measure and bore the holes for the dowels in both pieces.

3. Glue together.

4. Mount the keyhole brackets and hooks for hanging up.

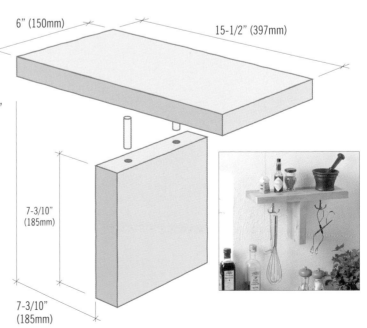

Music Center

I just have to admit it: I'm a nostalgic person who likes the old vinyl records!
The memories provide a happy and sentimental sense of comfort
...so wonderful! The entire record collection was in the cellar,
just waiting to be played again.

Since this stereo case was designed with the nostalgic person in mind, it makes sense that it was inspired by '80s stereo cabinets. These were often built with particle board, on which you could paste black veneer, and fitted with glass doors tinted with brown. We don't need to go that far. I wanted a piece of furniture that felt airier and lighter, but with the same functions.

Even this music center is rather big, but the "rail" design gives it a more open impression and the industrial wheels add a somewhat more modern touch. It was painted white with high gloss enamel to go with our house and has a box on the back to contain all the cords.

Now I can play Led Zeppelin's "Stairway to Heaven" at top volume — as long as no one else is at home!

A nostalgic person's stereo case was inspired by the '80s stereo cabinets and a radiator cover from the 1930s.

The back partition is far enough back so that a vinyl record in its sleeve has exactly enough space. There is a box for all the loose cords on the back, behind the partition.

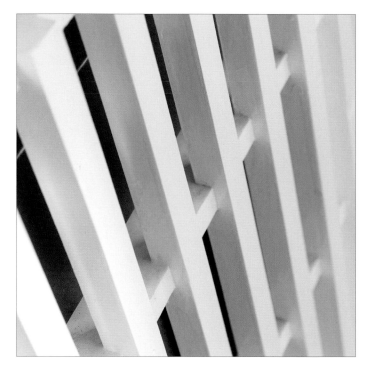

Materials

Sheets of 3/5" (16mm) MDF:

- **A.** 1 piece 13" x 17-2/5" (330x443mm)
- **B.** 1 piece 4-3/10" x 17-2/5" (110x443mm)
- **C.** 2 pieces, each 4-7/10" x 13" (120x330mm)
- **D.** 4 pieces, each 17" x 19" (440x490mm)
- **E.** 4 pieces each 4-7/10" x 6-7/10" (120x170mm)

Rails: 4/5" x 4/5" (22 x 22mm), 18 pieces, each 29" (734mm)

Glue

wood dowel pins

screws

4 Caster Wheels

Instructions

1. Cut all of the MDF pieces.

2. Screw and glue together A, B, and two sides C.

3. Screw and firmly glue the two D shelves, one under pieces A, B, and C and one over pieces A and C. Note that the D shelves should stick out 3/10" (7.5mm) on both sides of board C.

4. Join two sides E with wood dowel pins and glue.

5. Screw and glue one D shelf to the top.

6. Join the last two sides of E with wood dowel pins and glue.

7. Join the last D shelf with dowels and glue.

8. Cut the rails 29" (734mm) long. Cut and chisel out 3/10" (7.5mm) deep recesses for the casters.

9. Securely glue the rails spaced evenly apart. Clamp and let dry.

10. Attach casters.

Finishing

Cover any knots with wood filler. Apply two coats of primer, sanding lightly between coats. Sand and finish with one coat of enamel.

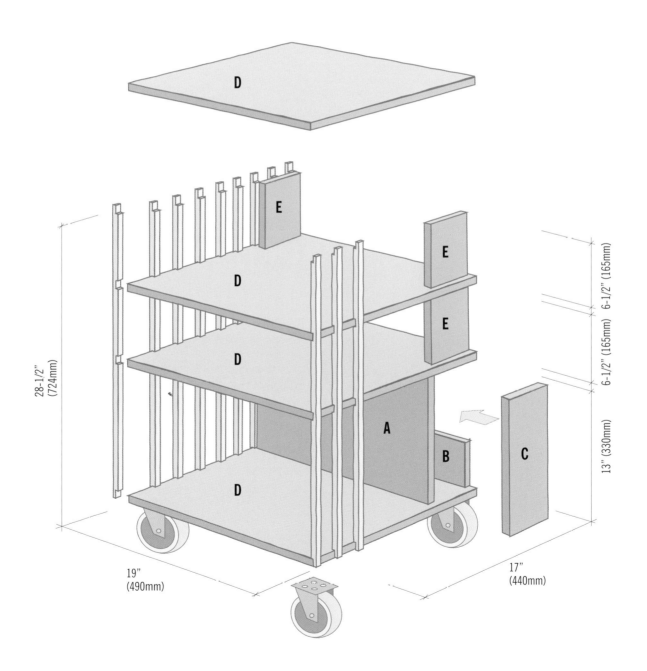

Bathtub Luxury

It doesn't happen all that often, but when we manage to find the time to sink into a fragrant bubble bath it feels so lovely to bathe in the light of a candelabrum.

We are lucky to have a bathtub deep enough to soak our shoulders and knees — at the same time. It's an extra bonus to be able to hang a glass of cold white wine on the shelf in front of me. When the children are bathing, we can fill the shelf with bath toys instead of the candelabrum and wine glasses.

The shelf is made with teak. It is pretty to look at, a fantastic material to work with, and it is moisture-resistant.

Materials

Teak boards: 1/2" x 2-3/4" (15 x 70mm), 3/20 (3.7mm)
6 wood biscuits: no. 0
Waterproof wood glue
12 screws

Instructions

1. Cut the boards: 3 pieces, each 31-1/2" (800mm) and 3 pieces each 8-1/2" (220mm). Note: Make sure that the measurements are appropriate for your bathtub.
2. Split two of the short pieces with the saw so that you have four pieces the same width for ends B. Glue them together two by two. Clamp and let dry. Sand.
3. Cut two end pieces C, 1/2" x 1/2" (15 x 15mm), out of the remaining short pieces of wood.
4. Mark the placement for the glass holders on the outer board A and bore a 2/5" (10mm) hole there. Use a router with a conformed cutter for hollowing out. Cut two slits into the hole.
5. Mark the placement of the screws and then bore out holes for the screws and plugs at the same time. Bore out wood plugs from a scrap piece with a plug cutter.
6. Screw and glue the shelf together. Put a bit of glue on the wood pins and tamp them down. Let dry.
7. Trim the wood plugs with the wood chisel.
8. Cut the shelf to the correct length; in this example 31" (785mm).
9. Join the end pieces C [1/2" x 1/2" (15x15mm)] at both ends with wood biscuits and glue. Clamp and let dry. Sand down the ends of the end trim rails so they are the correct length.
10. Sand the piece and then apply two coats of teak oil.

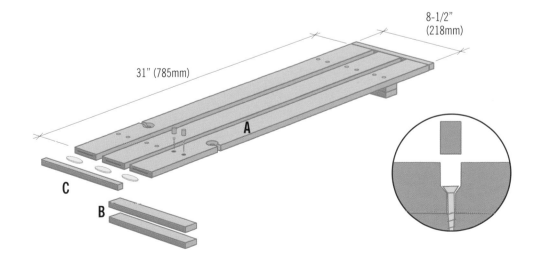

Planting Table

A planting table made so that the upper and lower "trays" are removable.
The folding stand makes it easy put the table
away after the plants have been repotted.

The assignment was to make a planting table suitable for my height. It should also be easy to move around, depending on the weather, wind, and changing moods.

When the children saw the table in its unpainted state, they thought that we had made a baking table. The idea wasn't completely wrong, but if you want to knead dough you'll need medium density fiberboard and probably a stronger stand. Our table is nothing more than a planting table painted with green linseed oil several times and then enameled with weatherproof "boat enamel" to resist soil and water.

The table is a slender piece of furniture that doesn't have to be protected in a dark corner of the yard. And, if some flowers need extra care in the winter, I can, if only temporarily, put the planting table in the kitchen.

The table has high edges so that you can have plenty of room while planting without knocking down the pots and fragile plants.

Materials

Plywood: 3/10" x 47" x 53" (7 x 1,200 x 1,350mm)

S4S planed rails @ 4/5" x 1-4/5", 11 yds. long
(22 x 45mm, 10m) and 3/5" x 3/5", 6 yds. long
(16 x 16mm, 5.5m)

2 carriage bolts, nuts, and washers

Screws

Thin rope: approx. 3 feet (1m)

Glue for outdoor use

Instructions for the table trays:

1. Cut out the piece of plywood:

   A. 1 piece 27-1/2" x 39" (700x1000mm)

   B. 1 piece 6" x 39" (150x1000mm)

   C. 2 pieces, each 6" x 27-4/5" (150x707mm)

   D. 1 piece 17" x 34-1/4" (430x870mm)

2. Round one of the corners on piece C with a jigsaw. Make a groove for the hand-hold by boring two holes with the hole saw and then cut with the jigsaw between them.

3. Cut rails E [3/5" x 3/5" (16x16mm)]. Glue and screw them along the edge around the underside of piece A. Do the same with D, but only on the long side. Don't forget to always counterbore into plywood.

4. Glue and firmly screw the back edge B the same way.

5. Glue and firmly screw sides C the same way.

6. Cut two 5" long (127mm) pieces from the thin rail. Glue and screw them in the corner between sides B and C.

7. Cut two 17"-long (430mm) pieces for the supports F [4/5" x 1-4/5" (22 x 45mm)]. Round the ends with a jigsaw and mount the supports with glue and then screw onto piece D.

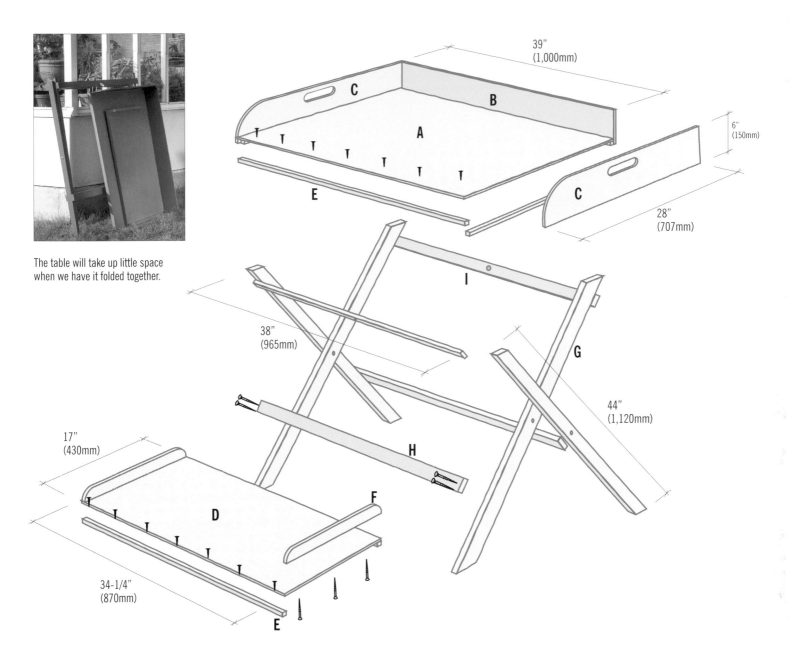

The table will take up little space when we have it folded together.

Instructions for the stand:

1. Cut the four legs G [4/5" x 1-4/5" (22x45mm)] so that the total length is 44" (1,120mm) and the angle of the ends is approx 55º.

2. Measure out the center point and bore holes in all four legs for the bolts.

3. Cut the two crosspieces H and I [4/5" x 1-4/5" (22x45mm)] that are 38" long (965mm). Counterbore, screw, and glue them on one pair of legs, with the lower one 10-1/2" (260mm) from the bottom and the top one 1-3/5" (40mm) from the top.

4. Join the other pair of legs the same way except that crosspieces H and I should be 36" long (920mm).

5. Place the pairs of legs together and join securely with bolts, nuts, and washers.

6. Bore a hole at the center of the crosspiece I and place a rope with a stop knot on the outside of the stay. Make sure that the knots are tied so that the rope is fully extended when the top tray is in place.

Window Shelf

We own a lot of decorative pieces
and all these little things each need a place.

Here's how it is with curtains. We don't have any talent in that regard and always try to work around the problem. In this case, the shelf becomes a part of the window, and the profile of the window frame is reflected in the shelf's edge. Finally, latex sealant does its duty.

It won't be long before the shelf is filled with objects. And I'm actually thinking about adding curtain holdbacks or hooks for café curtains or roman blinds in the window frame.

4. Place the shelf over the window case and screw it in from the top down into the case. Make sure that the case is well-anchored in the wall.
5. Apply latex sealant in the gaps to make it look as though the shelf has always been there and to help hold it in place.

Materials
Planed wood: 4/5" x 3-7/10" (22x95mm).
Make sure the piece is long enough to fit your window.
Glue
Wood dowel pins

Instructions
1. Cut shelf A approximately 5-1/2" (140mm) longer than the width of the window case. Cut off the front corner at a 45° angle. Profile cut all the edges except the one at the back.
2. Draw and then cut brackets B (see Schematic on last page). Profile cut them also.
3. Join the brackets with glue and dowel pins to the shelf so that they fit the window case precisely.

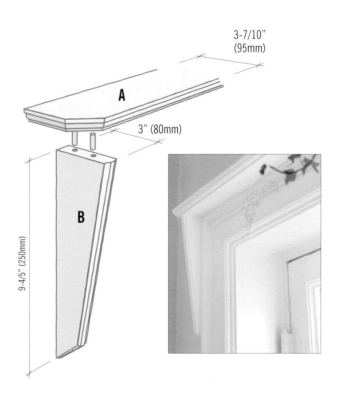

3-7/10" (95mm)

A

3" (80mm)

B

9-4/5" (250mm)

Loft Bed with Guardrail

Don't all children want to sleep high up near the ceiling? While visiting my grandmother's house every summer, my brother and I fought over who would get to sleep in the top of the bunk bed. Because I was the youngest — my brother was two years older than me — I had to sleep on the bottom...
Always.

When our daughter, Ida, was nine years old, it was time. She needed her own room to have some space to be peacefully alone or together with her friends, a zone free from parents and siblings.

A loft bed was at the top of her wish list — a bed to creep up into where she would just smile contentedly. Maybe a study corner would be nice also?

Of course, you can buy the furniture, but a room with a vaulted ceiling doesn't allow for any standard solutions. The bed needed to come out a bit from the wall; otherwise it would be too tight. So in that space, where the ceiling is the lowest, there are lidded containers instead. She can keep her secret things there, as well as her stuffed animals and other items that didn't have their own place previously.

Railings can be light and airy and stable at the same time so that dad can get his arm in it.

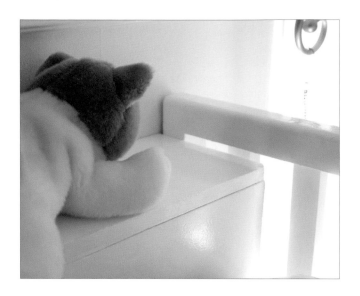

Pages 34-35, clockwise from bottom left:
Below the bed, Ida has a study corner where she can sit and read or write undisturbed.

The light streams in the room in the morning and her favorite cat has a place on the box by the window. Ida, on the other hand, prefers the thick, soft spring mattress.

The lid nearest the head pillow functions as a night table. Profile-cut trim that runs along all the walls becomes a fine transition between the wall and the ceiling and it goes with the bed's white, glossy woodwork. The trim effectively hides the spots we missed when the wall was repainted.

Ida chose the light blue color for the walls as well as a darker shade for the back wall. The posters in their red frames are actually hung a bit too high — just under the ceiling. Light blue and red? Together? Pretty, we think!

Loft beds normally have a ladder, but we choose instead to make a staircase. It is narrow and rather steep so it takes up minimal space on the floor — but, of course, it's easier to climb up than a ladder. A "staircase banister" made of two blocks and a rod minimizes potential wall damage over time.

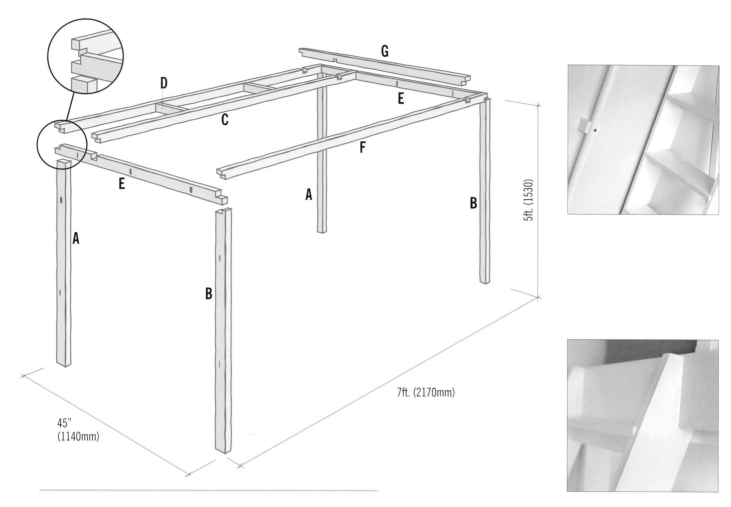

Materials

Dimensional lumber: 1-4/5" x 2-3/4", 59 ft. for the base (45x70mm, 18m); 1-4/5" x 4-7/10", 7ft. for the front edge of the frame (45x120mm, 2.17m); 1-4/5" x 1-4/5", 8 ft. for the railing (45x45mm, 2.5m)

Rails: 3/5" x 1-1/10", 17 ft. for railing (16x28mm, 5.2m); 3/5" x 1-4/5", 4 ft. for boxes (16x45mm, 1.2m); 3/5" x 1-4/5", 11 ft. for the stairs (16 x 45mm, 3.5m)

S4S Planed wood: 3/5" x 3-7/10", 23ft. for the stairs (16x9mm, 7m)

Particle board: 3/5" x 47" x 98-2/5" (16x1200x2500mm), just over 1-1/2 sheets (for the boxes).

Rod: 1-3/10" diameter for the stair railing (33mm)

Wood dowel pins

Wood glue

Screws

Wall plugs

Note that the measurements given above are not exact — you will need to adjust all measurements to fit the room in which you are building the bed.

Instructions

Base

1. Cut all the pieces for the base.

2. Join the four legs A and B with screws and dowel pins to the wall.

3. Screw and glue rails C together with the two short bars D.

4. Join crosspieces E with glue and screws above the legs and then join to rails C with glue and screws.

5. Join rails F and G with glue and screws.

Railing

6. Cut and join pieces H, I, J, and K with dowel pins and glue. The large board H is for the front edge, or frame, of the bed.

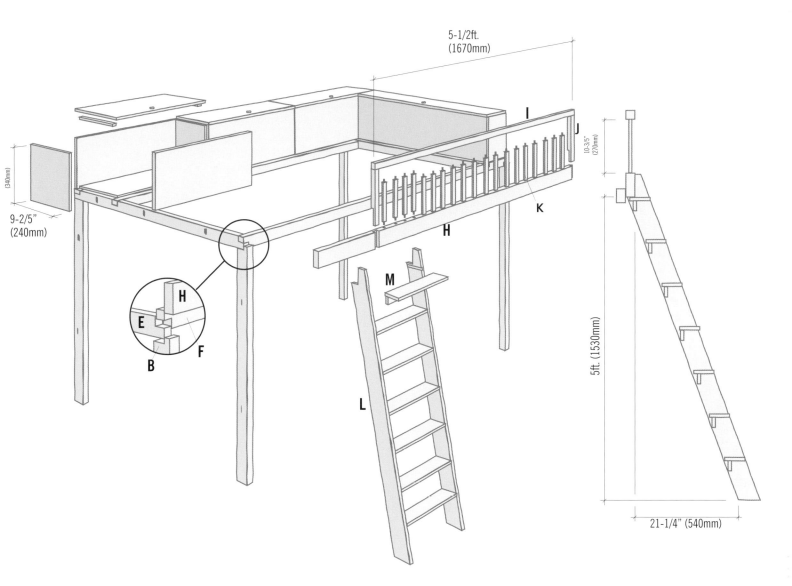

7. Glue and firmly screw board H with the rails on the bed. Note that railing H lies on a small "heel" of front leg B.

Stairs

8. Cut the side pieces L. Place them temporarily and mark where the top stair M should sit. Use a level to ascertain that the step is even.

9. Cut grooves in the side pieces L for the steps.

10. Cut steps M and screw them securely to the perpendicular supports under each step. Note that the support will be shorter than the step because the step will fit into the cut groove.

11. Join the steps with glue and screws.

12. Join the staircase with glue and long screws into the frame.

Boxes

13. Measure carefully and let the lumberyard cut all the pieces for you.

14. Glue and screw the boxes together. The lids should lie loosely on top of the boxes; rail supports under the lid insure that the lid won't slip around. Bore a hole in each lid big enough to stick a finger into so that the lid can be lifted off.

15. Put the boxes into place and attach them from underneath with some screws to the base.

Spackle, paint and let dry. The final step is to lift the bed into place.

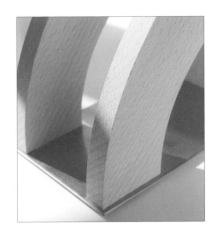

Book Ends

*Three irons from the nineteenth century were the only book ends
we owned that were actually functional.
Now the time had come to make some bookends that really work!*

The three book ends are shaped after the same principle. We used beech and sheet metal that we bought at the metal store in moderately-sized sheets. The wood parts were assembled with glue and dowels without any visible joins.

On two variants, it was possible to place a favorite book between parallel legs on the side with the front cover facing out.

Materials

Planed beech: 3/5" x 3-7/10" (16 x 95mm)
2/25" (2mm) thick sheet metal for the base: order pieces from
a sheet metal dealer or car repair shop
Glue
Wood dowel pins
Screws

Instructions

1. Sketch the pieces (see schematic on last page) and cut out
the wood parts with a figure saw.
2. Assemble pieces with wood dowel pins and glue. So that the
dowel holes will each be centered, hammer a small nail into
one part, nip off the head and press the parts together. Pull the
pieces apart, draw out the nail, and bore into the marked spot.
3. Grind and round the sheet metal edges with a file.
4. Measure the placement for the screws on the metal plate.
Bore and countersink.
5. Counterbore the wood pieces and screw together.
6. Glue felt to the underside of the metal base if desired.

*For option B, it is best to
glue the two arches that
the books lean against
before cutting them with
the figure saw.*

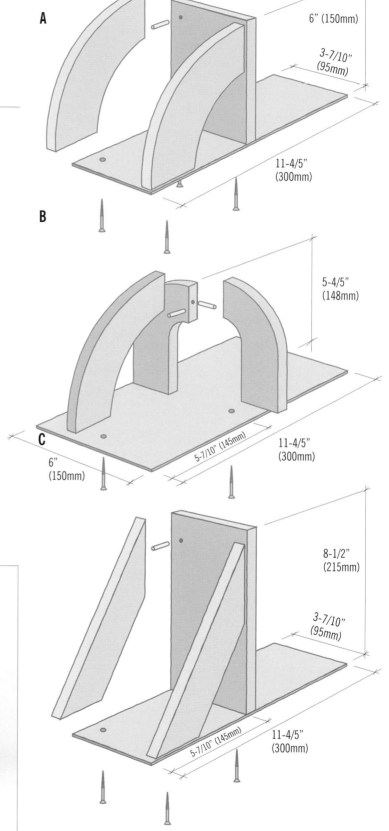

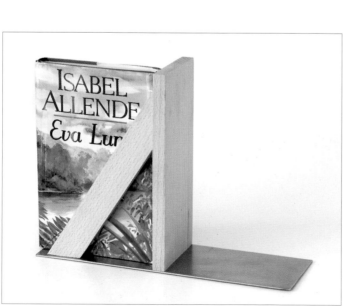

40

Window Ledge

Marble would look great with this project, but everything has its time and place. We already had basic marble window shelves. Now I wanted them to be deeper and wider, preferably white and very shiny like the window frame, to maximize the amount of light let in. We didn't want to damage the marble shelves because you have to be able to restore the original if your tastes change. The solution we found was thin plywood that, with a little glue, could be attached to the marble shelf. A thick trim for the front edge and on the sides makes the ledge look very solid and more massive than it is.

Materials

(length and width to fit the window)
Plywood: 1/4" thick (7mm)
Planed trim: 1" x 1-7/10" (27x43mm)
Wood glue
Threaded nails
Water-based construction adhesive
Latex sealant

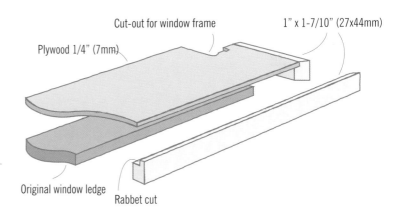

Cut-out for window frame 1" x 1-7/10" (27x44mm)
Plywood 1/4" (7mm)
Original window ledge Rabbet cut

Instructions

1. Cut out a paper template to fit the old window ledge precisely. Use it as a model and draw the shape on a 1/4" thick (7mm) piece of plywood. Add in the desired depth and width.

2. Cut out the plywood sheet.

3. Cut a rabbet along each trim bar, 1/4" deep (7mm) and 2/5" wide (10 mm).

4. Cut the trim pieces in a miter box to the correct lengths.

5. Glue and nail all the parts together.

6. Sand and then attach your new window ledge using a little contact concrete over the old one.

7. Spray latex sealant in the joins with the existing ledge so it will look as if the new window ledge has always been there.

Spice Rack

Spices are nice. Spices should be kept in a dark place, but it's also nice to have a pretty furnishing detail in the kitchen.

A stainless steel refrigerator. A stainless steel stove with its accompanying hood. For all the good food you'll be making in your kitchen, you'll need a spice rack for all your spice jars, which should follow the same style as your appliances. A suitably large, rustproof piece of sheet metal from the metal store is a coordinating link between the spice shelf and the stainless steel appliances in the kitchen — Beech panels with halving joints form the shelves — aligning it as near to the stove as possible, even if light does occasionally pass through between them.

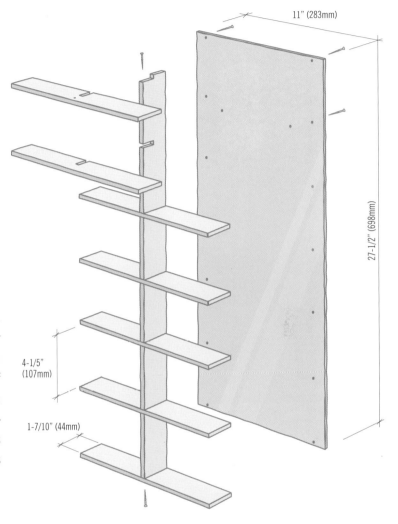

Materials

Stainless steel sheet metal: 27-1/2" x 11" (698x283mm); order to size from sheet metal store
Beech boards: 3/10" x 1-7/10", 10ft. (8x44mm, 3m)
Screws

Instructions

1. Cut the beech boards to the correct length. The vertical center piece is 27-1/2" long (698mm) and the seven shelves are 11" (283mm).
2. Cut and chisel out the halving joints in the vertical "wall" and the shelves — work especially carefully. Sand.

3. Measure the placement for the holes in the sheet metal. Bore and countersink the holes with a large drill.
4. Assemble the shelves and the center wall. Securely screw the top and bottom shelves onto the wall.
5. Lay the sheet metal into place and counterbore into the shelves.
6. Screw in the shelves from the back. The vertical wall is held in place by the shelves and does not need to be screwed in.
7. Bore two holes in the metal plate and secure the spice rack to the wall with screws.

Day Bed
with Drawers

We think that archival cabinets are nice. They invite us to be creative. It isn't just the adults who save their pictures here — even the children have their own drawers.

Quite often I find the children sitting by their file cabinets filled with keepsakes from their younger years. They will often ask me such questions as, "Mamma, do you remember when I made this drawing at daycare?"

We got tired of the cabinets being stacked on each other. It became a gigantic mess that was too heavy to push around when it was time to move the furniture.

We decided to divide the cabinet and use it as a daybed. A foam mattress was cut with a band saw (it was like cutting butter) to the right dimensions. The mattress is covered with a strong, dark gray wool fabric. The number of industrial caster wheels increased from four to six.

Maybe the furniture isn't any less clumsy to move around, but it looks more inviting where it stands now. That the cat has the same shade of gray as the mattress cover was not something we thought about before she found her favorite place.

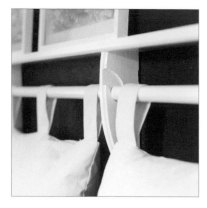

Above the bed we made a shelf with brackets for the wall pillows that hang around a wooden rod. The rods lie in recesses and are easy to remove.

The pillows are double sided with sweet sheep with small black eyes on one side and somber bone white fabric on the other. That makes it easy to change the bed's appearance. The shelf is basic but still has space for small things. We've even placed some framed school illustrations from the 1950s on it.

Day Bed

Materials

File cabinet/drawers for sketches

Particle board: 3/5" thick (16mm)

Edging trim: MDF painted trim 6/25" x 4/5", 36 ft. (6x20mm, approx 11m)

6 Wheels, including two with brakes: 3-3/10" diameter (85mm)

Glue

Nails

Screws

Instructions

1. Cut the two particle boards to size. Cut the edging trim with a miter saw, glue and nail the trim securely around the particle board sheets. The outer measurement must correspond precisely to those of the cabinet. Plane or sand down the trim to the thickness of the particle boards.

2. Firmly screw the particle boards onto the cabinet, one below and the other above.

3. Screw the casters on securely.

Shelf

Materials

Planed wood: 4/5" x 3-7/10", 10-1/2 ft. (21x95mm, 3.2m)

Wood rod: 1" diameter, 6-1/2 ft. (27mm, 2m)

Glue

Wood dowel pins

4 Keyhole fittings

Instructions

4. Cut the board for the shelf so that it is 7-foot-long (2100mm) and then plane down the width to size.

5. Draw a template for the brackets (see last page) and then cut out.

6. Cut out the recesses for the rod. The two outermost brackets should have a recess on one side only. Profile cut along the edge.

7. Chisel out the recesses for the keyhole fittings on the back of the brackets and mount them.

8. Join the brackets and shelf with glue and wood dowel pins or glue and screw them securely and then spackle.

9. Measure the exact length the rods should be and then cut them.

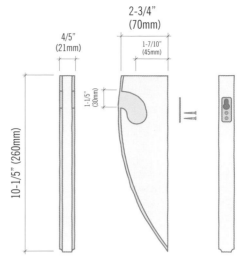

2-3/4"
(70mm)

4/5" (21mm)

1-7/10" (45mm)

1-1/5" (30mm)

10-1/5" (260mm)

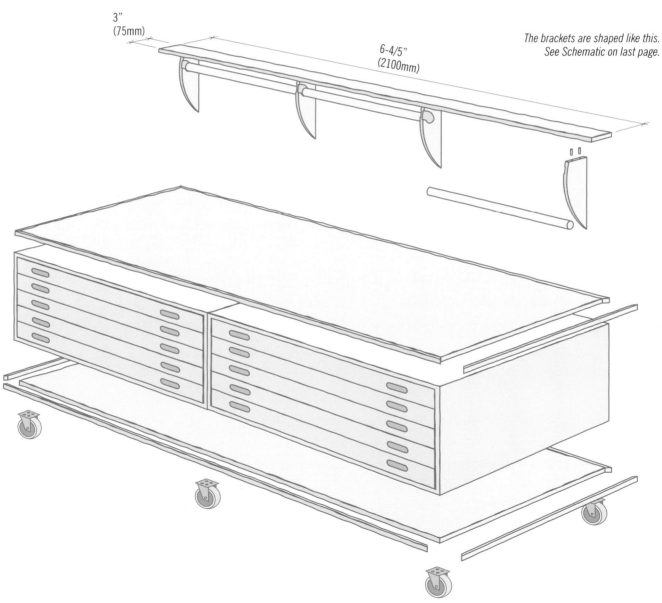

3"
(75mm)

6-4/5"
(2100mm)

The brackets are shaped like this.
See Schematic on last page.

Log Holder

It holds a lot of wood! We used to put a cassette into the fireplace and enjoy the heat from the fire all the better because of the energy savings.

Right now we let the fire go up the chimney at the beginning of November, but the coziness factor increases dramatically when we roast sausages, stick bread, and marshmallows later in the year.

Wood baskets are often low and don't have space for much wood, and tongs and other tools have to be stored separately. We wanted to build something taller to have space for more wood and the fireplace grill tools hanging at the side.

The wood holder was built with beech wood joined with glue and dowels. An extra bonus is the shelf at the top.

Materials

It can be somewhat difficult to obtain planed beech in the correct dimensions but pine will work equally well. You can also paint the log holder.

Planed wood: 1/2" x 1-7/10", 31 ft. (15x44, approx 9.5m), including shelf or approx. 7 ft. (6.5m) excluding shelf. See specifications below.
Legs (A): 4 pieces each 3 feet (910mm)
Crossbars at sides (B): 6 pieces each 8-1/2" (215mm)
Crossbars front and back (C): 4 pieces each 12" (310mm)
Shelf (D): 8 pieces each 14" (360mm) — the total measurements for the shelf are 12-4/5" x 14" (325 x 360mm). Note: If you are using a different material for the holder or plan on painting it, it will be easier to cut the shelf from sheets.
Supports under the shelf (E): 1 piece 10-4/5" (275mm) split lengthwise to 2 pieces 1/2" x 4/5" (15x22mm)
Wood dowel pins
Screws

Instructions

1. Cut all the pieces.

2. Bore, join with dowel pins, and glue all the pieces together for the frame.

3. Bore in the frame pieces and crossbars, join with dowel pins and glue. Note that the crossbars at the bottom are longer than those at the top to minimize the risk that the wood will fall through.

4. Glue the pieces for the shelf together. Lay rails under and over the shelf and hold together with clamps as you glue them and then place the shelf in a bar clamp. That will hold the pieces in place and the shelf will be level.

5. Screw and glue the two supports to the underside to prevent the shelf from falling in. Place the supports so that they fit precisely into the frame.

6. Sand the shelf well because it may not be completely level or smooth after gluing.

7. Screw the shelf securely into place on the supports going through the supports under the shelf.

8. Cut the hooks from small pieces of beech and secure them with glue and dowels to one of the frame's crossbars so you can hang up the fireplace tools.

9. Finish with oil or lacquer.

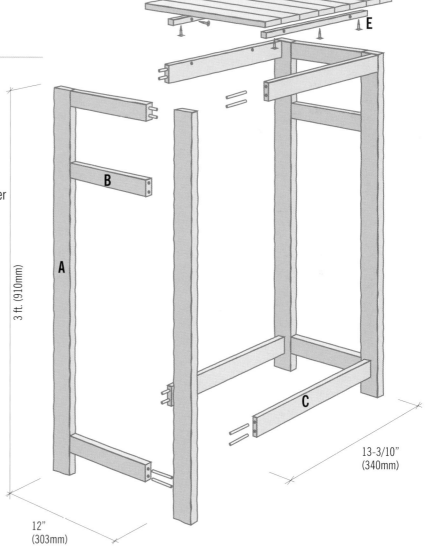

3 ft. (910mm)

13-3/10" (340mm)

12" (303mm)

Light Holder

When I was little, it used to snow at the beginning of December and it was so light and pretty after a dreary November.

That is how I remember it, but the reality is different. What we wanted to achieve with our arced candle holder was a warm and inviting façade in a gray and dark December. And, if I do say so myself, I think we've succeeded. The candle holder was measured to fit our French doors. It is in place year round and integrated with the window décor. Ordinary Christmas tree lights are attached to the pegs spaced along the arc. And I continue to dream of a white Christmas…

The façade is symmetrical with three French doors so we needed three candle holders.

Materials

Medium density particle board: 3/5" thick (16mm) — adjust the size
to fit your window.
Round dowels: 3/10" diameter, 4 ft. (8mm diameter, 1.2m)
Glue
Christmas lights

Instructions

1. Draw the arched frame (the radius in our case was 37 and 40 inches
[950 and 1,020mm]). Make a compass by attaching a pencil to one
end of a string and nailing the other end down at a suitable distance for
drawing a short radius. First draw the line for the smaller radius and
then lengthen the cord by about 2-4/5" (70mm) and draw the line for
the larger radius.

2. Cut out the arches.

3. Measure and bore 16 holes 2/5" deep (10mm) evenly spaced on
both arches

4. Cut 16 pieces of dowel, 2-4/5" long (70mm) each.

5. Glue all the pieces to both arches at the same time; set in a press
and let dry.

6. Cut out two small masonite pieces in the shape shown below in the
drawing and attach them to the window niche.

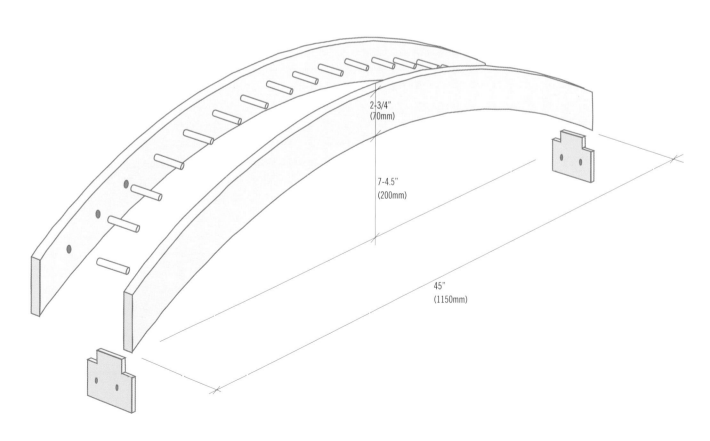

2-3/4"
(70mm)

7-4.5"
(200mm)

45"
(1150mm)

Candelabrum

In the mid-twentieth century, it was very popular to do fret saw work. The do-it-yourself pages in the weekly magazines gave the guys at the kitchen table ideas.

A modern electric fret saw doesn't take up any more space than a sewing machine. It can be set up on the kitchen table as an ideal work space for the carpenter-wanna-be without a work shed.

For me, fret sawing is synonymous with Christmas. Surely the Christmas spirit calls for cutting out some pieces for a box, a book end, a little coffee tray, a small shelf, a frame, or name plates for the herbs in the greenhouse, right?

Materials

Plywood: 1/5" x 19-1/2" x 19-1/2" (4 x 500 x 500mm)
Round dowels: 1/2" diameter (15mm), cut to desired length
6 candleholders: (available in hobby shops).
A hook, a chain, glue, and a screw
Craft paint

Instructions

1. Draw (see schematics on last page) and cut out pieces. Make the holes by boring a small hole and then inserting through the circular saw blade and cutting.
2. Cut the dowels, glue and then screw them securely into the round plate without a center hole.
3. Cut a 1/5" wide (4mm) groove in the bottom of the candleholders so that they can be fitted to the plywood.
4. Glue the candleholders firmly into place.
5. Temporarily assemble the candelabra before you paint it, in case you have to adjust the holes a bit.

Mount and hang up the candelabrum when it's time. When Christmas is over, take the candle holder apart so it fits into the Christmas box in the attic.

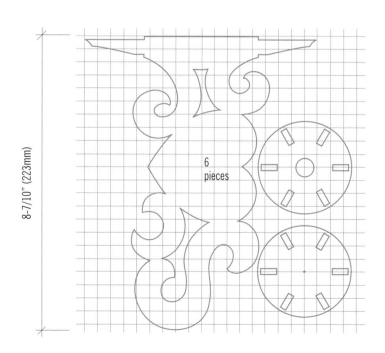

8-7/10" (223mm)

6 pieces

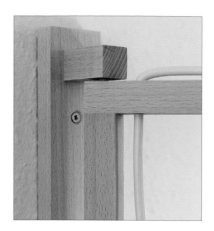

Swing Lamp

You saw them in the 1950s — lamps with an accordion arm.
Inspired by the "cool" '50s, we made our own variation.

Our lamp is simpler and perhaps more modern. It is made with beech and has a moveable arm. The idea was to use a ceiling or window lamp that you have at home or buy a new, simple lamp.

The lamp can be varied many ways: the style of the lamp shade, the length of the arm, the type of wood, etc. You can also make an even simpler version without the swinging arm. And, why not hang several in a row over the desk or any other place that needs strong lighting.

Materials
A cheap ceiling/window lamp: (ours is from IKEA)
Plug, electric fittings, and a cord
Planed wood: 4/5" x 4/5", 3 ft. (21x21mm, approx. 1m)
— we used beech, but pine is an excellent substitute for the arm. Paint the pieces if you want.
Planed wood: 1/2" x 1-7/10", 10" (15x43mm, 265mm)
Wood dowel pins
Screws

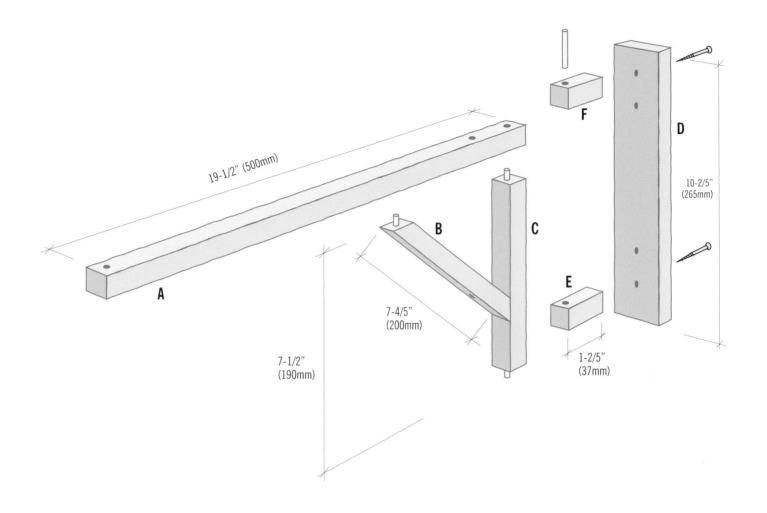

19-1/2" (500mm)

A

B

7-4/5" (200mm)

7-1/2" (190mm)

C

F

D

10-2/5" (265mm)

E

1-2/5" (37mm)

Instructions

1. Cut pieces A, B, and C.

2. Following the drawing, bore three holes for the cord: two on the top piece A and one in the diagonal support, B.

3. Join the three pieces for the arm with glue and dowel pins.

4. Cut board D for the wall bracket. Bore four holes in it, two for blocks E and F and two for hanging.

5. Cut out blocks E and F and bore holes in them. Use a bore slightly thicker than the dowels so that it doesn't jam in the holes. On the lower block (E), the hole should not go all the way through, but, in the top block (F), bore the hole completely through. Screw and glue the blocks to the wall bracket D.

6. Bore a hole at the bottom of part C and glue a dowel pin into it; make sure pin doesn't stick out more than 1/5" (5mm).

7. Bore a 1/5" deep (5mm) hole upwards to the interior of A. Use a bore slightly thicker than the dowel so it will go into the hole easily.

8. Put the arm into place and put a dowel pin through the hole in block F and end near the bottom of the hole in piece A. Trim the dowel exactly level with the edge of the hole. When trying out the lamp, all you have to do is lift the lamp's arm. Then the dowel will stick up 1/25" – 2/25" (1-2mm) and will be easy to grab and remove.

9. Thread the cord through and install the electrical fittings and plug.

Tray Table

I have to admit something — I have breakfast served to me in bed every morning. Freshly brewed coffee and, quite often, fresh rolls. It even comes on a "silver tray"!

My friends are a bit jealous and their husbands don't want to talk about it. But, if truth be told, I think that I get breakfast only so I will be a more pleasant mother and wife.

I had my grandmother's old and beautiful silver tray and we made a small frame for it. The height is just right for our rather high bed. After breakfast, I can simply fold it up and put away the frame and tray.

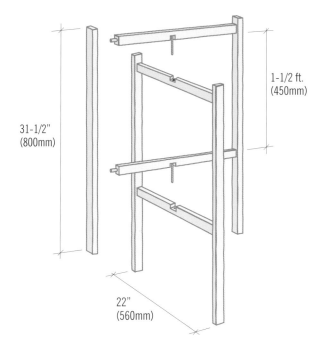

31-1/2"
(800mm)

1-1/2 ft.
(450mm)

22"
(560mm)

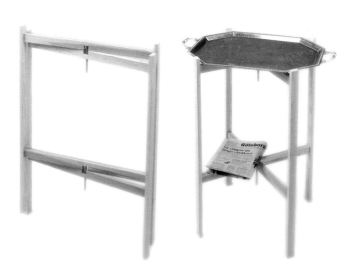

Materials

Planed wood: 1/2" x 1", 9'8" (15x27mm, approx. 3m)
Planed wood: 4/5" x 1", 8 ft. (21x27mm, approx 2.5m)
Rods: 2/5", 9-4/5" long (10mm, 250mm)
Wood dowel pins: 3/10" diameter (8mm)
Wood glue

Instructions

1. Cut the 4 legs [1/2" x 1" (15x27mm)] and the four pieces for the crossbars [4/5" x 1" (21x27mm)] to the correct length. The length of the crossbars depends on the size of the tray to be used.
2. Cut and chisel halving joints to a so-called "blade cut" in a cross at the center of the rails for the crossbars.
3. Cut the rods into two pieces each 4-1/2" (120mm).
4. Bore holes for the rods centered on the blade cuts. On both of the top rails of the cross, the hole should not go all the way through. Glue the rods there. In both of the lower pieces, the holes should go through completely.
5. Pin and glue the pieces together with two of the crossbars through one pair of the legs.
6. Repeat with the other pair of legs but don't forget to assemble the frame before the last leg is glued into place.

Child's Bed

*A bed to grow up with! Short and snug when
the child is little, and, with new, longer sides,
the bed can be used for many years.*

I think there is a little Astrid Lindgren feeling in this bed. It could easily have been in Madicken's room, in the big wood house in Junibacken.

The bed is constructed in the classic, romantic style with high ends and traditional beadboard painted with high gloss, white enamel.

The proportions of the bed during the early years, when it is quite short, make it feel snug and cozy. As the child grows, you only have to lengthen the sides and bottom while keeping the head and footboards in proportion.

To tell the truth, we lengthened the beds a bit too early, just so that the children's tall parents could have a chance to lie in them comfortably and read stories.

*This is, of course, a typical girl's room,
but the bed is equally suitable for a boy,
so why not paint it green or blue?*

The bed is now 6-1/2 feet long (two meters). The dolls have moved down to the basement and a dream catcher hangs on the wall. Today the bed accommodates a girl who has gotten tired of stories and reads the "Harry Potter" book series all by herself. The next step for the bed is in the guest room in the basement, but that can be put off for a couple more years.

Materials

Legs A: planed wood 1-4/5" x 1-4/5", 13 ft. (45x45mm, 4m)

Crown molding D: planed wood 3/5" x 3-7/10", 6-1/2 ft. (16x95mm, 2m)

Crossbars B and bottom slats J: planed wood 4/5" x 1-4/5", 91 ft. (22x45mm, 28m)

Head and Foot boards C: Beadboard 1/2" x 3-7/10", 65 ft. (12 x 95mm, 20m)

Trim E: Untreated pine molding 3/5", 13 ft. (16mm, 4m)

Cover strips F: planed rails 6/25" x 3/5", 6 ft. (6x16mm, 1.8m)

Mounting rails I: planed wood 3/5" x 1-1/10", 3 ft. (16x28mm, 1m)

Support rails H: planed wood 4/5" x 4/5", 8-1/2 ft. (22x22mm, 2.6m)

Bed sides G: glulam 7/10" x 8-7/10" x 51" (18x220x1300mm), 2 pieces

Bottom of bed K: peg board 4/25" x 31" x 52" (4x790x1,325mm)

4 Bed hook fittings

Glue, wood dowel pins, and screws

Instructions

1. Cut the crossbars B and legs A for the ends. The lower crossbar consists of two boards that are glued and screwed together as an inverted T. Insert dowel pins and glue the legs and crossbars for both bed ends.

2. Cut and glue/nail the beadboard C on both sides of the bed ends in crossbars B.

3. Cut the crown molding D and profile cut it all around. Join the pieces on the ends with dowel pins and glue.

4. Miter cut the covering rails E and glue/nail them securely.

5. Cut the covering rails F and glue/nail them over the gap between the beadboard and the crossbars on the outside of the bed ends.

6. Draw the shape of the bed sides G on the glulam sheets and cut. Trim the supports H, glue and screw them securely in the lower edge of the long sides.

7. Cut the four mounting rails I. Chisel the recesses for the bed fittings in the boards and in the legs.

8. Securely join the mounting rails in bed sides G with long screws without using glue. That makes it easy to remove the boards later for longer sides when the child has grown out of the bed.

9. Fit the bed together. Make sure that the corners between the ends and the sides are squared and then screw the slats J into the support rails (H) without glue.

10. Cut and fit the pegboard K.

11. Paint the bed unassembled. Begin by covering all the knots with wood filler. Prime twice, smooth and paint with one coat of enamel.

When the bed is to be lengthened later, it will need new sides and more slats. The mounting boards with the bed fittings can be moved to the new long sides.

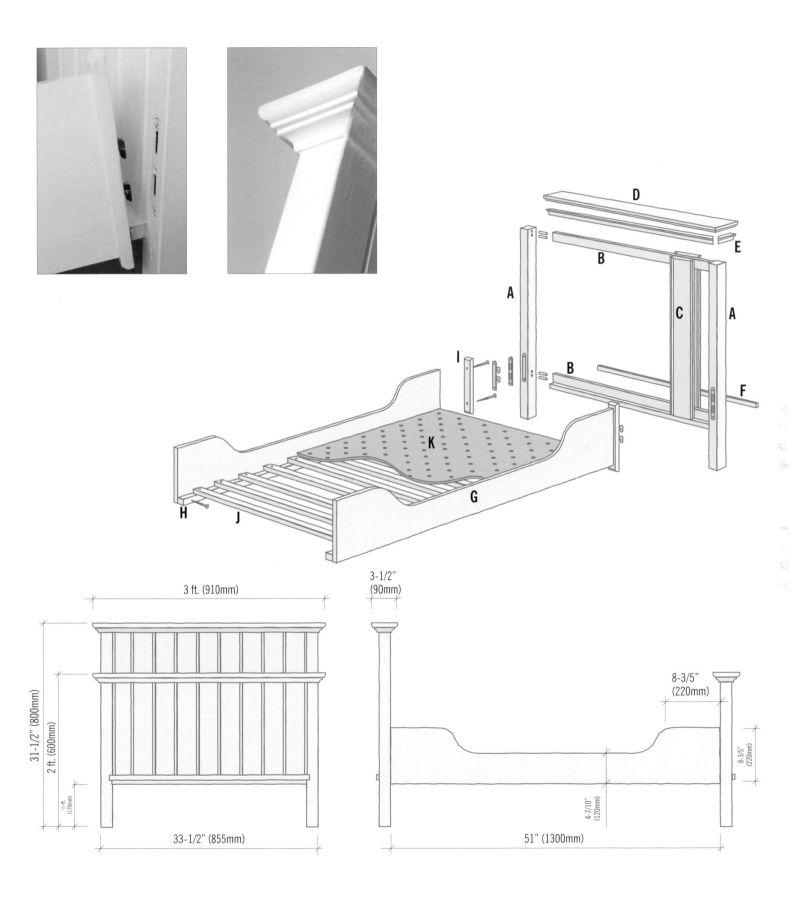

D

E

B

A

C

A

I

B

F

K

G

H

J

3 ft. (910mm)

3-1/2"
(90mm)

31-1/2" (800mm)

2 ft. (600mm)

½ ft.
(170mm)

33-1/2" (855mm)

8-3/5"
(220mm)

8-3/5"
(220mm)

4-7/10"
(120mm)

51" (1300mm)

Stairs

Our greenhouse, with its four meters in ceiling height has a floor surface of only 16 square meters. The stairs down from the kitchen to the little paradise couldn't take up a lot of space. It needed to feel as airy as the room itself.

It was the easiest construction possible – white painted stair risers and stained and enameled steps that will withstand many trips up and down.

It was while we were building these stairs that we discovered a milling machine or "biscuit" machine as they say in folk dialect. It is a very good tool that doesn't cost too much. It made it quick and easy to assemble the parts for the stair risers without any screw heads showing. Joining pieces with biscuits and glue is more flexible than with dowels.

There were some details to take into consideration when choosing the color. The brown for the stair treads was chosen because of the mud and dirt but the color also wouldn't clash with the brick wall and tile floor. The white of the stair risers reflects the white around the base of the house.

Every now and then the stairs become a shelf, a place to sit, and then stairs again. And the way down to paradise can be bordered by plants of various sorts.

Materials

All measurements should be adjusted so stairs fit your house.
Planed dimensional lumber:
1-4/5" x 3-7/10", 5 ft. (45x95mm, 1.5m): 2 pieces
1-4/5" x 4-7/10", 3 ft. (45x120mm, 1m): 11 pieces
1-4/5" x 2-4/5", 7 ft. (45x70mm, 2.1m)
Wood glue
20 wood biscuits
22 screws: 4/25" x 3" (4x75mm)
2 corner brackets
5 French wood screws and washers: 2/5" x 4-7/10" (10x120mm)

Instructions

1. Cut the side boards for the stringers A [1-4/5" x 3-7/10" (45x95mm)] from the dimensional lumber. The ends should have a 45° angle with a rebate cut for the wall bracket D at the top end.

2. Cut the triangles B [1-4/5" x 6-7/10" (45x170mm)] for the risers to hold up the stair treads. Note that the lowest risers must be trimmed on one corner.

3. Join the triangles with biscuits and glue. Clamp and let dry.

4. Cut the wall bracket D [1-4/5" x 6-7/10" (45x170mm)]. Mount it securely to the wall. In our case, the distance between the top edge of the bracket and the floor/ground is 38-1/2" (980mm).

5. Secure the completed stringers to wall bracket D with French wood screws and corner brackets.

6. Cut the treads C [1-4/5" x 4-7/10" (45x170mm)]. Plane or cut away approx. 1/2" (5mm) on one side of the board to eliminate the rounded edges. Glue the parts together two by two to the risers with the planed or cut surfaces facing each other. The top step has three boards.

7. Attach treads C with screws.

8. The frame of the stairs in the photos was painted white and the treads were stained and enameled.

The greenhouse, which is directly off from the kitchen, is in a class of its own among the items we've built. The plants can continue to thrive long into the fall. It is a bit cooler, of course, but the greenhouse extends our summer by a couple of months. We try to spend as much time here as possible, serving supper or taking a coffee break, repotting a plant, or just sitting and relieving the soul from stress and hurry.

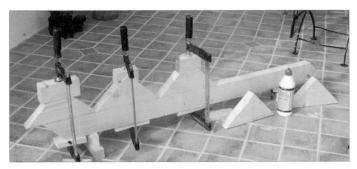

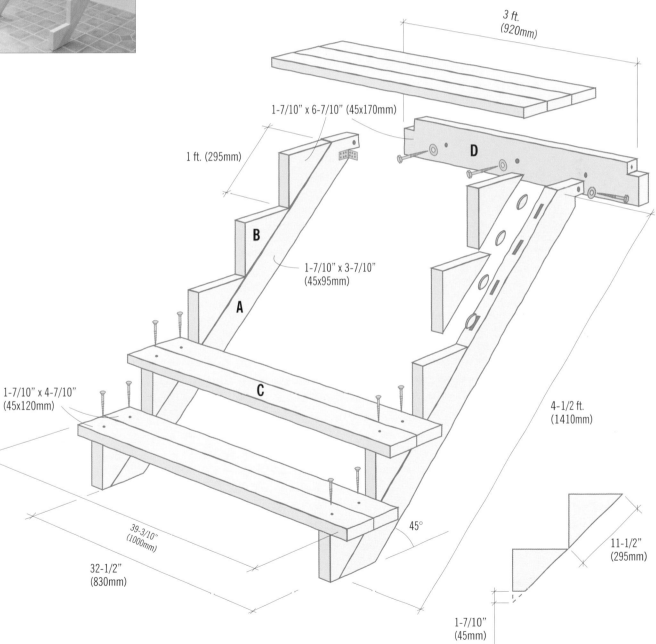

3 ft.
(920mm)

1-7/10" x 6-7/10" (45x170mm)

1 ft. (295mm)

D

B

1-7/10" x 3-7/10"
(45x95mm)

A

C

1-7/10" x 4-7/10"
(45x120mm)

4-1/2 ft.
(1410mm)

39-3/10"
(1000mm)

45°

32-1/2"
(830mm)

11-1/2"
(295mm)

1-7/10"
(45mm)

65

Garage Doors

Our family is very interested in cars!
Making the garage bigger, no matter how expensive, was necessary.
Now there is plenty of space for two cars.

The garage has two openings — one that leads out to the street and another towards the backyard. We have the latter so we can stand in the grass, among the apple trees and birches and clean the chrome.

Usually you have to buy ready-made garage doors because they are heavy, difficult to build, and impossible to hang straight. However, doors at the shops are expensive and we wanted to deny a myth — you can build garage doors yourself at a fraction of the cost at the store. With a couple of simple tricks it goes more quickly than you would dare to believe.

The secret with our doors is that you build them right there in one piece. Then you simply cut them at the center and open the doors.

Our garage is in the center of town but it feels as if it is in the country. The exit is made over a little, grass covered hill. I think it has to do with one of our many dreams: to live in the country sometime and to have a big red barn with room for cool antique cars and a gray Ferguson tractor from the 1950s.

The doors are painted with red
linseed oil, a color that dries
slowly but is very durable.

Materials

A + B: lumber 1-4/5" x 5-3/10", 10 ft. (45x135mm, 3m): 3

C, D, and L: planed wood 4/5" x 2-3/4", 10 ft. (22x70mm, 3m): 4

E, F, G, and J: boards 1-4/5" x 4-7/10", 10 ft. (45x120mm, 3m): 3

K: planed wood 4/5" x 1-4/5", 6-1/2 ft. (22x45mm, 2,050mm)

H: tongue-and-groove paneling 1-1/10" x 4-7/10", 6-1/2 ft. (28x120m, 2,050mm): 18

11 French screws for mounting the frame: 2/5" x 4-7/10" (10x120mm)

Strap hinges: 4 pieces, approx. 29-1/2" long (750mm), including French wood screws and machine-threaded screws with nuts and washers.

Handles, Barn door locks

2 Sliding bolts

4 Corner brackets

Screws: 1/5" x 3" (4.3x75mm)

Instructions

1. Cut boards A and B [1-4/5" x 5-3/10" (45x135mm)] for the frame. Cut and chisel out the mortise and tenon for the corner joints.

2. Assemble the parts of the frame in the door opening with screws the right size for the walls.

3. Cut and screw together rails C and D [4/5" x 2-3/4" (22x70mm)] 1-1/5" (30mm) from the front edge. Begin by boring the holes on the inside of the rails for the screw heads in the frame.

4. Cut the two long, horizontal boards E and F for the door [1-4/5" x 4-7/10" (45x120mm)] so that they fit between rails C in the frame. Screw in the four corner brackets and then place and securely screw in boards E and F on them. The front sides of boards E and F should lie edge to edge with the front of the C rails.

5. Trim the diagonal boards G [1-4/5" x 4-7/10" (45x120mm)] and attach them with clamps at the correct angle against boards E and F. Mark the cutting lines on each board E and F. Take down all the boards and cut out the notches for diagonal pieces G on boards E and F.

6. Screw boards E and F in again. Join the diagonal boards G in the correct placement once more. Now, on the diagonal boards, draw the shape of the notches made in boards E and F. Take down the diagonal boards and cut them.

7. Set up the diagonal boards G, making sure that they fit exactly and won't be either too loose or too tight. Attach to boards E and F with a screw at each end.

8. Cut and screw the tongue-and-groove panels H. Begin with the two in the center, plane off the markings on them and place them with 1/5" (5mm) in between. The boards should cover C and D.

9. When all the tongue-and-groove boards are mounted, screw in the hinges. Use the French wood screws in the frame and the machine-headed screws with the nuts and washers in the door.

10. Remove the corner brackets. Cut the door through the gap at the center.

11. Mount the sliding bolts at the top and bottom of the inside on one half of the door, and one batten K [4/5" x 1-4/5" (22x45mm)] over the gap between the doors on the outside of the other. We recommend profile cutting along K.

12. Securely screw in the two wood blocks J for the barn door lock on the inside of the tongue-and-groove paneling, at the center of the door.

13. Install the barn door locks in blocks J on the door.

14. Cut a drip rail L [4/5" x 2-3/4" (22x70mm) for both halves of the door and screw it in securely at the lower edge.

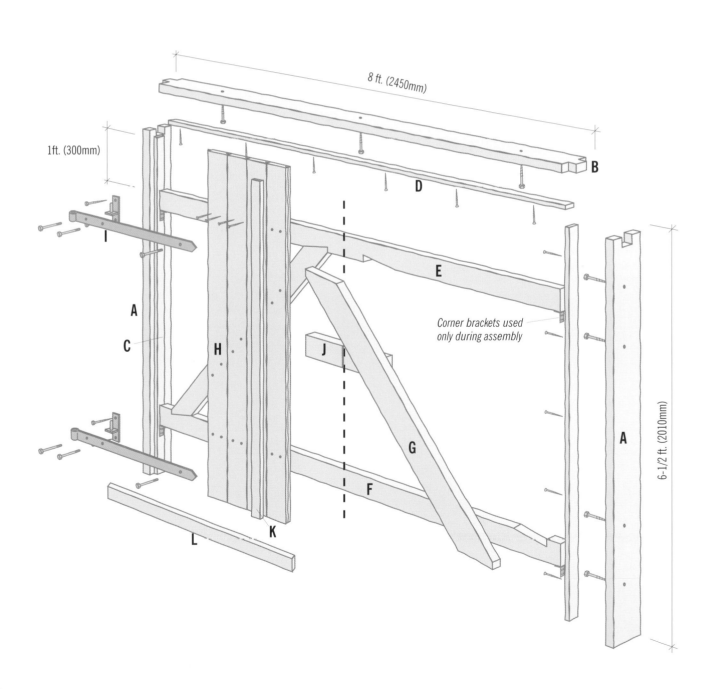

8 ft. (2450mm)

1ft. (300mm)

B

D

I

E

A

Corner brackets used only during assembly

C

H

J

A

6-1/2 ft. (2010mm)

G

F

L

K

Long Bench

Grill parties, christenings, birthdays, and children's parties — there are so many opportunities that call for extra, occasional places to sit.

How many odd chairs have we carried up and down the basement stairs when a true bench is much more flexible. The construction is simple: two collapsible trestles and two long planks. Heavy rope with knotted ends holds the trestles in the right position.

The bench works just as well if you are alone or with a few others; for example, for a hot chocolate break while the fall leaves rustle, or as a "liar's bench" facing out from a pleasant side of the house. But it is not made for long, social sittings — for those parties we get out the garden furniture.

Materials

Pressure-treated wood:

5-7/10" x 1-4/5", 10 feet (145x45mm, 3m) – 2 pieces
3-7/10" x 1-4/5", 1-1/2ft. (95x45mm, 500mm) – 6 pieces
1-4/5" x 1-4/5", 1ft. (45x45mm, 300mm) – 5 pieces
4 strong hinges
Wood glue for outdoor use
16 screws: 4/25" x 3" (4x75mm)
Rope: 8ft. (2.5m)

Instructions

Seat

1. Cut the three crossbars A [1-4/5" x 1-4/5" (45x45mm)] that are 1 ft. long (290mm).

2. Glue and screw the crossbars securely onto the two long boards B, one on each plank 10" (250mm) in from the ends on B, and one at the center. The spacing between boards B should be 1/2" (15mm).

Trestle

1. Cut bars C [1-4/5" x 1-4/5" boards (45x45mm)] so that they are 1 ft. long (290mm). Cut or plane one long side to an approx. 73° angle.

2. Cut two legs D [3-7/10" x 1-4/5" (95x45mm)]. Note that they should be angled at approx. 73° on one end.

3. Glue and screw one leg at each end of bar C. Countersink the screws.

4. Cut the center leg E. It should be slightly shorter than the other two. Note that it should also be angled at one end.

5. Place leg E between the assembled legs D and attach to bar C with two strong hinges.

6. Bore a hole (3/5" [16mm]) in the outer legs D. Pull the rope through as shown in the drawing and tie each end so that the legs can come out far enough.

7. Make another trestle the same way.

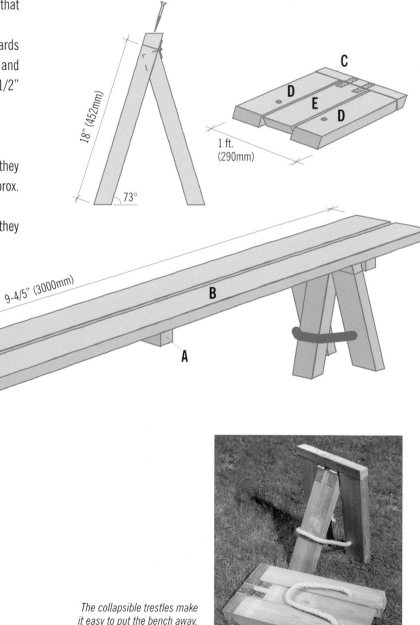

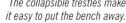

The collapsible trestles make it easy to put the bench away.

Holder for Knife Sharpener

The mountain of scrap wood from the bench is shrinking and we found out that things we barely even knew we wanted have suddenly found the right place in the kitchen.

A holder for a knife sharpener makes the tool easy reach when the tomato skins suddenly feel hard to slice.

A few square inches/centimeters of a beech wood block, a figure saw, one hole, two screws, a suitable place, and we always have sharp knives forever.

Materials

Scrap blocks of wood from the bench

Instructions

1. Draw the shape on the block of wood.
2. Bore a hole for the sharpener.
3. Cut piece following the drawn lines and sand.
4. Bore holes for the mounting screws.

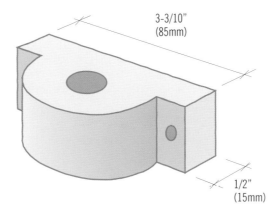

3-3/10"
(85mm)

1/2"
(15mm)

Kitchen Table

A square table with enough room to seat eight, spaciously, and with a bit of weight to it... It isn't easy to find such a table in stores.

The kitchen is the heart of the home and in our house it is the natural gathering place for both family and friends. I wanted to have a rustic kitchen table with a big, generous tabletop that would function equally as well for meals as for homework and puzzles. The new table has plenty of room for eight people but four or even two can be just as comfortable there. For everyday use, we simply push the schoolbooks aside and set the table for dinner. In contrast to a rectangular table, a square table lets everyone around the table communicate. We decided to paint our table white so that the kitchen would be as bright as possible.

We built the table in the basement, without considering the narrow basement stairs that the table would have to come up. Eight-year-old Hilda noticed the problem before her father did. Anders grumbled, took the table apart, and assembled it later in place in the kitchen.

The corner blocks make the construction strong while the mounting blocks, with tongues that stick into grooves in the crossbars, hold the table top in place.

Materials

Tabletop: dimensional lumber 1-4/5" x 5-7/10", 5 ft. (45x145mm, 1500mm) — 10 pieces
Supports for the top: dimensional lumber 1-4/5" x 1-4/5", 3-1/2ft. (45x45mm, 1100mm) — 2 pieces
Legs: 3" x 3", 2-1/2 ft. (75x75mm, 740mm) — 4 pieces
Crossbars: 1-3/10" x 3-7/10", 4 ft. (34x95mm, 1,160mm) — 4 pieces
Corner blocks: 1-3/10" x 3-7/10", 7" (34x95mm, 180mm) — 4 pieces
Mounting blocks: 4/5" x 1-4/5", 2-2/5" (22x45mm, 60mm) — 12 pieces
Glue
Screws
4 French wood screws with washers
(For the glue jacks: dimensional lumber 1-4/5" x 1-4/5", 29-1/2 ft. [45x45mm, 9m].)

Instructions

1. Plane the legs A to 2-3/4" x 2-3/4" (70x70mm) and the crossbars B to 1-3/10" x 3-7/20" (34x85mm).

2. Cut a 1" long (25mm) tenon at each end on crossbars B. The length of the crossbars between the tenons should then be 3-1/2 ft. (1110mm). Chisel a 1/2" deep (12mm) groove in the crossbars (see drawing).

3. Bore and chisel out the holes for the crossbar tenons in the legs.

4. Glue legs and crossbars together and clamp. Web clamp if possible. Cut 4 pieces each 3-1/2 ft. (1110mm) to place between the legs at the opposite end of the assembly so it will be easier to keep the underside of the table squared.

5. Cut the corner blocks C and bore three holes in each. Glue and securely screw the corner blocks (see detail picture) to make the table well-supported and stable. Use the French wood screw at the center.

6. Using a planer, plane the boards for table top D that will be glued together to measurements 1-2/5" x 5-3/10" (35x135mm).

7. Glue the boards in the homemade glue jacks (see page 75). Hit the wedges forcefully so that the pieces are firmly in place.

8. When the glue has dried, glue and screw the supports E. Cut the pieces to the right length, 4-1/2 ft. (1350mm), and sand.

9. Put the table top in place. Cut 12 mounting blocks F (4/5" x 1-4/5" [22x45mm]) with a groove, push them into the housing in the crossbars and screw on the table top.

How to glue the table top together:

Build a glue jack for gluing the table top together. Use 1-4/5" x 1-4/5" (45x45mm) dimensional lumber. Cut 2 boards 5-1/2 feet long (175cm) and 4 blocks 1/2-foot-long (15cm). Glue and screw the blocks at ends of the boards. Cut 8 wedges. Lay the boards for the table top that will be glued between the blocks. Cut 20 blocks and place one on each board in the table top and, over them, a board 5 feet long (150cm). Press the top boards together and the glue jacks with screw clamps so that the table top won't bow when it's put into the press. The blocks are used to prevent the boards from being glued to the table top.

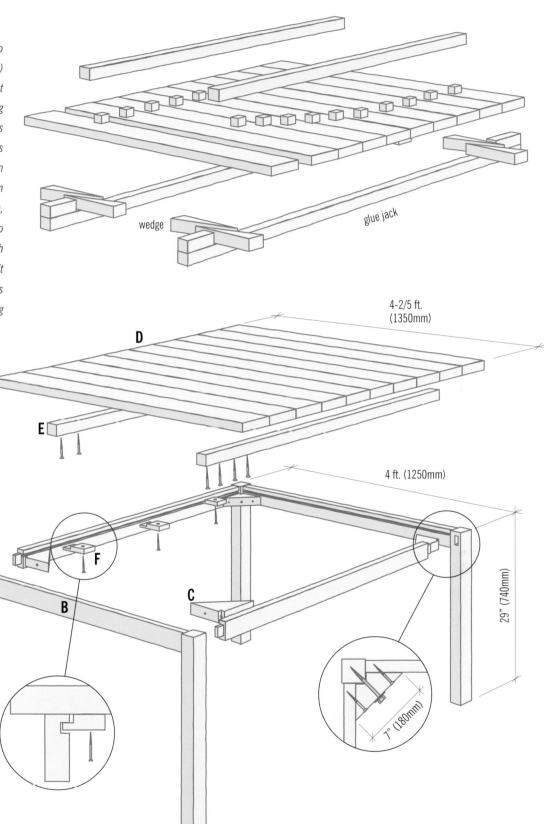

wedge

glue jack

4-2/5 ft. (1350mm)

D

E

4 ft. (1250mm)

29" (740mm)

F

C

B

A

7" (180mm)

Bar Table

Stand and work, sit and drink a glass of wine — a useful table that you can easily move around.

Sometimes the table is a workplace in the office and sometimes it's a bar table in the kitchen where the dinner guests are served aperitifs. Work or pleasure — in the best case either/or. The table is 3-1/2 feet high (105cm) and the shape is classic with stable straight legs and a table top made of medium density fiberboard.

I can stand at the table and look at old slides, the children sit and draw and play while I work — and we can also toast each other here.

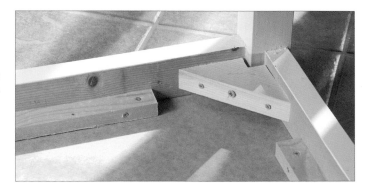

A block in every corner, three strong screws and glue make the table very stable. The table top is screwed into supports on the top edge of the frame. If you want to use glulam instead of medium density fiberboard, the top can be mounted with furniture brackets.

Materials

Table top E: 3/5" (16mm) MDF sheet, 27-1/2" x 27-1/2" (700x700mm)

Legs A: planed wood 3" x 3", 3-2/5 ft. (75x75mm, 1035mm) – 4 each

Crossbars B: planed wood 1-1/10" x 2-3/4", 2 ft. (28x70mm, 600mm) – 4 each

Corner brackets C: planed wood 3-7/10" x 1-1/10", 1/2 ft. (95x28mm, 180mm) – 4 each

Support for table top D: rails 1" x 1", 9-4/5" (27x27mm, 250mm) – 4 each

Glue

screws

Instructions

1. Plane legs A to 2" x 2" (55x55mm) and the crossbars B to 1-1/10" x 2" (28x55mm).

2. Cut a 1" long (25mm) tenon at each end of the crossbars. The length of each crossbar between the tenons is then 21-1/2" (550mm).

3. Bore and chisel the mortises for the crossbar tenons in the legs.

4. Glue the four legs and the crossbars and then clamp. We recommend also web clamping. Cut 4 pieces each 21-1/2" (550mm) to place between the legs at the opposite ends of the assembly, so that it is easier to keep the base of the table top squared.

5. Cut corner blocks C and bore 3 holes in each. Glue and screw the corner brackets in securely (see detail drawing) to make sure the table will be very durable and stable.

6. Glue and screw the supports D for the table top into the top edge of the frame pieces and screw in firmly. (If you are using glulam instead of MDF, attach with furniture braces instead.)

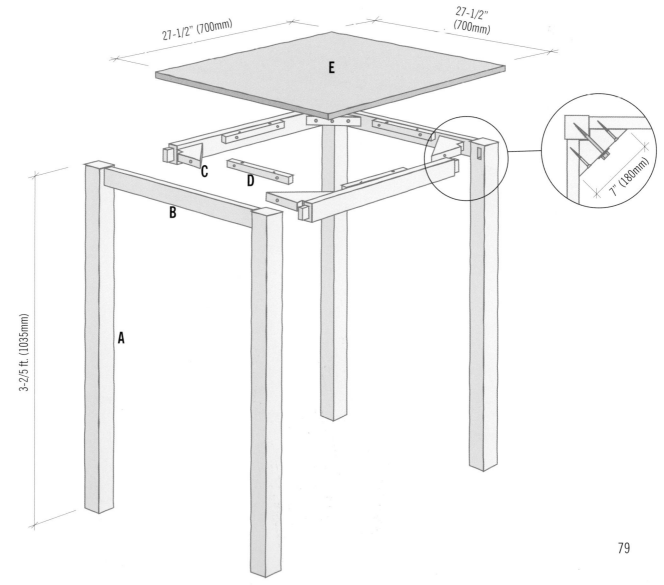

Shed

The general feeling of the backyard was, in one way, the main motivation when the project started — a project that ended up solving a real dilemma posed when getting the car into the garage.

The garage was filled up with stuff — a high pressure washer, the lawn mower, flower pots, and tires — that was constantly in the way when the cars had to be driven in or out. We definitely needed a storeroom.

The long, narrow, empty space along the back led to the construction of a shed that was also long and narrow. Later, of course, the shed had to swallow masses of stuff. A dividing wall, half of the shed's width, made room for a bracketed shelf for flower pots. The outer wall, together with the gridded window, gave a nice feeling to the room.

The shed has two doors — a narrow one where the gardening tools and pots can go in and a double door for bicycles and the wheelbarrow. Another positive aspect of the shed's long and narrow shape is that it's an excellent place to store lumber and ladders. And, back in the garage, the cars are now free from the risk of being scraped by someone walking by with a ladder under her arms.

Materials

6 Concrete plinths

Aggregates and gravel

Lumber for the base frame and roof beams:

dimensional lumber 1-4/5" x 4-7/10", approx. 41-1/2 yds. (45x120mm, approx. 38m)

Floorboards: dimensional lumber 1-4/5" x 3-7/10", approx. 16 yds. (45x95mm, approx 15m).

Cover boards for the base frame: cut wood 4/5" x 4-7/10", 11 yds. (21x120mm, 10m)

Wood frame: dimensional lumber 1-4/5" x 2-3/4", 142 yds. (45x70mm, approx. 130m)

Floor and roof: tongue-and-groove roof cladding 7/10" x 3-7/10", approx. 273 yds. (17x95mm, approx 250m)

Outer panel lumber: cut wood, 1" x 9-4/5", 295 yds. (25x150mm, approx. 270m)

Cover battens: cut wood 1" x 1-1/2", 273 yds. (25x38mm, approx. 250m)

Casings, etc.: cut wood 1" x 5", 65-1/2 yds. (25x125mm, approx 60m)

Triangular rails: 2" x 2", 11 yds. (50x50mm, approx. 10m)

Screws, washers, and nuts for the plinths: 12 pieces

4 nail plates

Corner brackets: 4 large size for the base frame and 24 small size for the roof beams

14 beam shoes

Roof foot plate, 6 yds. (5.6m)

10 gutter hooks

Gutters and drainpipe

Roofing underlayment, 13 square yards

Roofing felt, 13 square yards

Shingle nails

Roofing glue

Nails

Screws

Instructions

1. Dig holes for the plinths. Make sure the holes each have a solid base. Fill with hard packed aggregates and gravel high enough so that the plinths will stick up about 2" (5cm). Set plinths into the holes, making sure that each is straight.

2. Cut the pieces for the flooring frame A (1-4/5" x 4-7/10" [45x120mm]) and nail together. The long sides are cut for halving joints with nail plates and, in the corners, join the frame using corner brackets or halving joints.

3. Check the frame with a level and then attach the frame to the plinths with bolt-through screws, washers, and nuts. The distance between the plinths' metal connectors is 2-3/4" (70mm), so you'll need some blocks on the inside.

4. Cut the floorboards B (1-4/5" x 3-7/10" [45x95mm]) and attach them to the base frame with beam shoes.

5. Fill in the holes around the plinths with gravel and pack down well.

6. Attach a cover batten C (4/5" x 4-7/10" [21x120mm]) on the outside of the long sides of the frame so that the screw heads and connectors on the plinths are "countersunk."

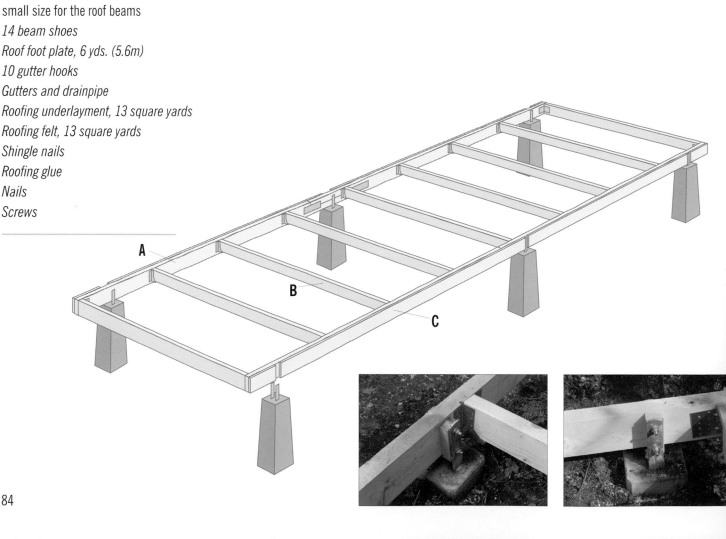

7. Build the bearing walls with the upright boards D, the crossbars E, the noggins F and the hammer bands G (total dimensions 1-4/5" x 2-3/4" [45x70mm]). It is easier but more expensive to screw the pieces together than to nail them. Check squaring throughout with a level. Be extra careful about the crossbars which will hold the whole structure straight.
8. Cut the roof beams H (1-4/5" x 4-7/10" [45x120mm]). Cut the housing where they will lie on the hammer bands. Attach the roof beams with corner brackets.
9. Screw or nail boards I 1-4/5" x 2-3/4" (45x70mm) between the roof beams aligned with the wall boards.

10. Cut and screw the horizontal supports J (1-4/5" x 4-7/10" [45x120mm]) between the roof beams and the standing boards on the right side.
11. Lay floor K with the tongue-and-groove roof cladding (7/10" x 3-7/10" [17x95mm]) with the smooth sides up. Nail into the grooves or tongue so that nail heads are not visible.

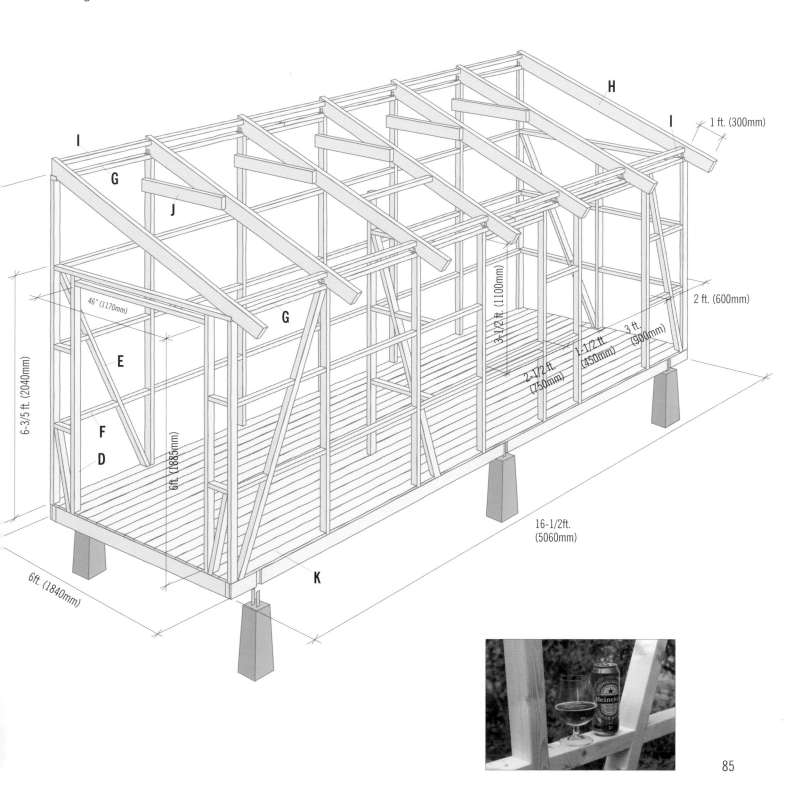

85

12. Clad the shed with panel boards L (1" x 6" [25x150mm]). Look at the grain on the ends of the wood and turn the wood so that the core is inwards. Trim the wood diagonally along the lower edge so water can run off. Cut the top edges of the panel boards for the gable after they have been set in place.

13. Nail the roof underlay M (tongue-and-groove roof cladding 7/10" x 3-7/10" [17x95mm]). Cut the tongue off the lowest board and begin from the bottom. Mark and cut off the ends when all the roof boards have been nailed.

14. Cut and screw the triangular rails N above the underlay along the sides of the gable and the highest part of the roof.

15. Mount the hanging hooks O. Countersink them in the roof cladding boards with a circular saw.

16. Nail the roof footplate P along the lowest side of the roof.

17. Lay the underlayment Q, following the manufacturer's instructions.

18. Attach the window frames and door frames (see pages 89 and 90) in line with the panels using screws. Use the level to ensure that the top and bottom pieces are horizontal and the side pieces are vertical. Place small pieces of masonite between them if necessary. Make sure that the diagonal measurement is the same on the window and the door respectively.

19. Paint the panel boards L and the cover battens R (1" x 1-1/2" [25x38mm]) once before the battens are placed over the gaps in the panels. Nail the cover battens so that the nails go between the panels and into the boards. Trim the covering battens at an angle across the lower edge so water can run off. Paint all the trimmed ends by hand. Take into consideration where the window and door frames will be. Finish painting the entire panel.

20. Lay the roofing felt S. Follow the manufacturer's instructions carefully.

21. Paint all the frames T, knot boards U, wind boards V, and the water boards X before they are cut and put into place. Use cut wood (1" x 5" [25x125mm]). Measure, cut, and nail but don't forget to paint the ends of the wood by hand. The knot boards should be trimmed diagonally along the lower edge for water runoff. Paint everything one last time so that all the nail and screw heads are covered by paint.

22. Hang the window, which you can construct yourself, see p. 91.

23. Build the door in situ, see notes on p. 89.

24. Mount the gutters and drainpipe.

Hilda was quite focused when it came to painting the shed – from the green linseed oil paint to the red doors with black iron details and white trim. A little bit of the country in the city.

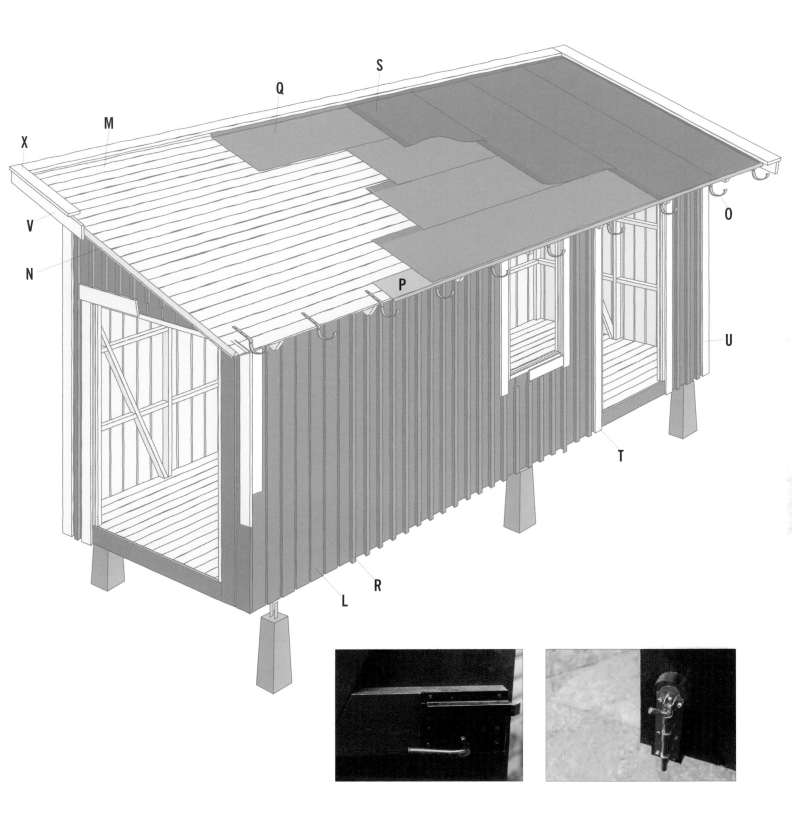

Doors

Materials

Dimensional lumber: 1-4/5" x 3-7/10", 9-3/10 yds. (45x95mm, 8.5m)

Planed wood: ½" x 1-3/10", 5 yds. (15x34mm, 4.7m)

Unfinished tongue-and-groove: 7/10" x 3-7/10", 23 yds. (17 x 95mm, 21m)

Strap hinges: 2, approx 19-1/2" long (500mm), including screws, washers, nuts, and French wood screws

Handles

Barn door lock

4 corner brackets

Screws

Instructions

1. Cut the wood (1-4/5" x 3-7/10" [45x95mm]) for the frame A. Cut and chisel out the mortise and tenon for the corner joints.

2. Mount the frame in the door opening with long screws.

3. Cut and screw together the rails B (1/2" x 1-3/10" [15x34mm]) 7/10" (17mm) from the front edge.

4. Cut the two crossbars C (1-4/5" x 3-7/10" [45x95mm]) so that they fit between the rails on the frame. Screw in the four building fasteners and set up. Screw the two boards tightly on them.

5. Roughly trim diagonal board D (1-4/5" x 3-7/10" [45x95mm]) and fix it at the right level with clamps at board C. Mark where the transverse boards will be cut. Take down all the boards and cut out the notch for the diagonal board in board C.

6. Screw the transverse boards together again. Put the diagonal board in the right place once more. Now draw the notch on the transverse boards onto the diagonal board. Take down the diagonal board and cut.

7. Set up the diagonal board, making sure it fits exactly, without any looseness or tightness. Attach it in crossbars C with a screw at each end.

8. Cut and screw in the tongue-and-groove panels E. Begin at the center and make sure that the outermost two are the same width.

9. When all of the tongue-and-groove boards are in place, screw in the hinges, using French wood screws in the frame and screws with washers and nuts in the door.

10. Remove the fasteners and open the door.

11. Attach the barn door lock on a piece of board, G, on the door.

12. Cut a drip rail F from the tongue-and-groove paneling and screw it firmly along the lower edge.

You can construct double doors in the frame in almost the same way (see pages 67-69 for the garage doors).

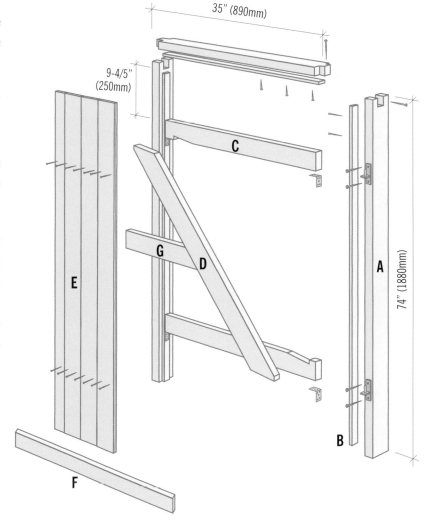

Materials

Frame, A: dimensional lumber 1-4/5" x 3-7/10", 4 yds. (45x95mm, 3.6m)

Window sash, frame, B: dimensional lumber 1-4/5" x 1-4/5", 3-1/2 yds. (45x45mm, 3.4m)

Grids, C: planed wood 1-3/10" x 4/5", 2-2/5 yds. (34x22mm, 2.2m)

Drip moldings D: quarter rounds 2/5" x 2/5", 30" (9x9mm, 660mm)

6 pieces glass: ea. 3/25" x 12" x 11-1/2" (3x308x295mm)

2 hinges

2 window latches

Window putty

Wood glue

Wood dowel pins

Nails and screws

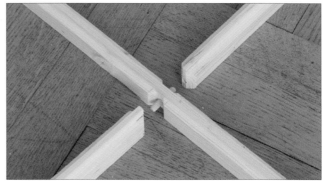

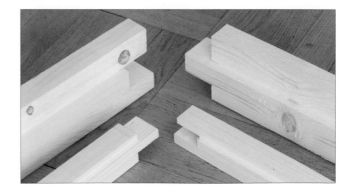

Windows

Instructions

1. Cut a groove 2/5" x 1-4/5" (10x45mm) in the wood (1-4/5" x 3-7/10" [45x95mm]) for frame A.

2. Cut the pieces for the frame. Sand down the groove in the under part of the frame (between the side frames) so that it leans a little downwards and outwards. Cut and chisel the mortise and tenons for joining the corners.

3. Cut or chisel the recesses for the hinges in the frame and screw them in tightly.

4. Counterbore and screw the frame together.

5. Mount the frame aligned with the panel using long screws. Lay small pieces of masonite in between if necessary. Use a level to insure that the parts of the frame all are true horizontally and vertically. Also make sure that the diagonal measurements match on the frame.

6. Cut a groove for the glass 3/10" x 2/5" (7x10mm) in the wood (1-4/5" x 1-4/5" [45x45mm]) for the window sash of frame B.

7. Cut the pieces for the window sash frame. Cut and chisel out the mortise and tenons for joining the corners.

8. Cut a groove for the glass 3/10" x 2/5" (7x10mm) on two sides of the wood (1-3/10" x 4/5" [34x22mm]) for grids C.

9. Cut the grids and bore holes for the wood dowels in the grid ends and in the sash frame. The standing grids have two long wood dowel pins that go straight through.

10. Mount and glue the pieces of the window sash; clamp and let dry.

11. Nail and glue a quarter round D as a drip rail at the bottom of the window frame.

12. Cut or chisel out the recesses for the hinges, double checking the placement. Screw in the hinges. Hang the window sash and make sure it is set in slightly. Sand and adjust as necessary.

13. Prime the sash and frame. Set in the glass, securing it with small tacks and putty.

14. Hang the sash and paint it.

15. Attach the window latches.

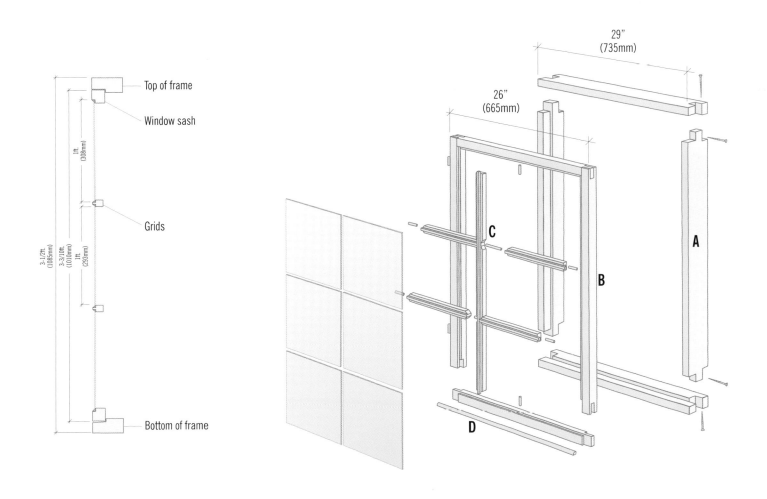

91

Gate

It had to do with keeping watch on Ida – then 2 years old – when her little sister came into the world. With the addition of a gate, the terrace became a limited but exciting area for Ida to run around in.

A gate also meant that I didn't need to worry about Ida falling down the stairs into the yard. Of course, we could have made something temporary, but the gate proved to be necessary for several reasons. Not the least of which was making the terrace feel comfortable and cozy.

We chose a simple, classic design with railings in the gate. But we made the design somewhat simpler to draw the eyes to the cross on each half of the gate. The crosses also function as braces to stabilize the construction, so we can open and close the gate easily for many years to come.

These days the gate is usually open and the girls, their friends and the dog run up and down the terrace steps. But, if someone little comes to visit, the gate stays closed and the adults can relax.

Materials

Dimensional lumber: 1-4/5" x 2-3/4", 4 yds. (45x70mm, 3.6m)

Cut wood: 1" x 1-1/2", 4 yds. (25x38mm, 3.6m)

Wood dowel pins and glue

2 hinges

Gate latch/handle

Instructions

1. Cut the pieces of the frame from the dimensional lumber: A: 2 pieces each 3 ft. (900mm) and B: 3 pieces each 2 ft. (600mm).

2. Cut and chisel out 1-1/2" long (40mm) tenons on the crossbars B. To make the gate more stable, cut a slit in each tenon and carve a little wedge. The wedge should be small enough that it just fits when you clamp the standing boards and crossbars together.

3. Bore and chisel out the mortises for the tenons in the standing boards A.

4. Temporarily assemble the frame and measure the exact center on the standing rails C. Also mark the crossbars D where they cross each other.

5. Cut all the rails C and cut and chisel the tenons on them.

6. Cut and chisel the halving joints on the crossbars.

7. Bore and chisel the holes in the lower and center crossbars B for the upright rails C.

8. Mark and bore holes in the crossbars D as well as the top and center horizontals B for the wood dowel pins that will secure the cross.

9. Glue all the parts at the same time. Clamp and let dry.

10. Attach the hinges and handle.

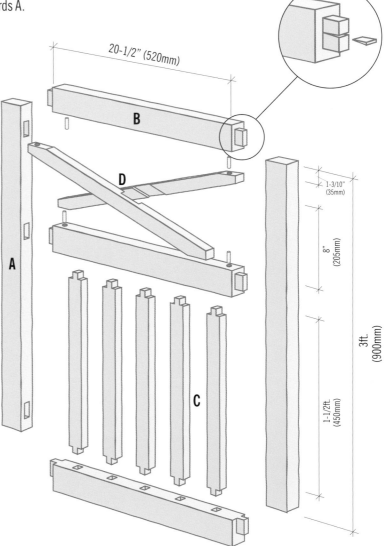

Herb Shelf

What do I do with the fresh herbs when I come home from the store? "Hang them in the window," said one of my daughters.

Precisely — on an oak shelf with four holes for glass pots in a lovely shade of blue. It has become a fine still life offering a bit of everything, especially a handy place for the herbs by the stove. The pots remind me of little flower bouquets in the summer like the hyacinths at Christmas.

Materials

Planed oak: 2/5" x 3-7/10", approx. 2 ft.
(9x95mm, approx 700mm)
Wood biscuits
Wood glue

Instructions

1. Cut the piece for the shelf (length to fit window) and brackets.

2. Measure the spacing and diameters for the holes for the pots and make the hole with a hole saw.

3. The base should be 4/5" (20mm) from the edge. Mark placement for the screws and, with a drill, bore the holes for the screws and form the plugs at the same time. Bore out the wood pins with a pin cutter from some scrap wood.

4. Screw and glue the shelf together. Place a bit of glue on the wood pins and tamp them down. Let dry. Trim the pins with a wood chisel.

5. Bore a hole diagonally upwards on the back of the brackets.

6. Sand the shelf and coat with oil.

7. Measure where the shelf will be placed; drive in nails and trim nail heads.

8. Hang the shelf on the nails.

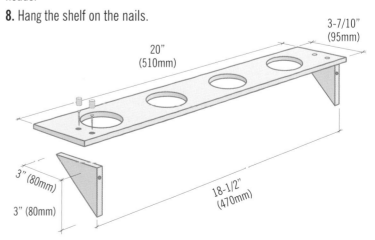

Desk

A T-shaped desk allows space for several work stations. The table was constructed according to our particular needs, but it can easily be designed to reflect your own taste, needs, and space. And why not paint it with rich colors?

We wanted to have a desk designed for the office that would maximize the space. We needed places for the big pieces of equipment as well as the small ones so several people could work at the same time. That was the idea behind the T-shaped desk which made two good work spaces. If need be, it can even be expanded for three.

The children don't have, at least up to now, computers in their own rooms. The girls often keep me company at the desk where they can play, surf the web, or chat. We've lifted the CPU box off the floor and onto shelves that we attached to the desk with screw-in rods.

The children surf the web, at least for the time being, under our watch (but we still read everything the girls write).

Sitting for many hours in front of the computer requires a good working position. The solution is a table top sawn at a 45-degree angle in one corner. Shoulders and back are spared when the arms can rest on the table.

Materials

Sheet A: MDF 3/5" x 35-1/2" x 27-1/2" (16 x 900 x 700mm)

Sheet B: MDF 3/5" x 35-1/2" x 70" (16 x 900 x 1,800mm)

Sheet C: MDF 3/5" x 35-1/2" x 39" (16 x 900 x 1,000mm)

Sheet D: MDF 3/5" x 23-1/2" x 10-1/2" (16 x 600 x 270mm)

Legs, E: cut wood 3" x 3", 6-1/2 yds. (75 x 75mm, 6m)

Crossbars, F: planed wood 1-3/10" x 2-3/4", 13-1/2 yds.
(34 x 70mm, 12.5m)

Corner braces, G: planed wood 1-3/10" x 3-7/10", 31-1/2"
(34 x 95mm, 800mm)

Support rails, H: planed wood 1-3/10" x 1-4/5", 2 yds.
(34 x 45mm, 2m)

Mounting rails: cut wood 1" x 1", 5 yds. (25 x 25mm, 4.5m)

Screws with washers and nuts: M8, 5 pieces

4 corner brackets

4 screw-in rods: M8, ea. 27-1/2" (700mm)

Nuts and washers for rods: M8, 12 pieces

Dome-head nuts: M8, 4 pieces

Wood glue and screws

Instructions

1. Cut the legs E, taking some off at the top, and plane them to 2-1/5" x 2-1/5" (57x57mm). Adjust the length of the legs as necessary.

2. Bore and chisel out the holes for the crossbar tenons in the legs.

3. Cut all the crossbar pieces F and cut the tenons on the ends that will be glued into the legs.

4. Glue together all three parts for the base, constructing each section separately, and then web clamping. Cut appropriate length struts to maintain the correct distance between the legs and let them sit in the clamp between the legs at the opposite end when gluing so that the structure is straight. Clamp and let dry. Glue and screw the corners together without the legs.

5. Cut the corner blocks G (1-3/10" x 3-7/10" [34x95mm]) and bore three holes in each. Glue and screw them into place. The corner blocks provide stability for the desk.

6. Cut the two extra support rails H (1-3/10" x 1-4/5" [34x45mm]) to go under the largest desk top. Glue and screw in the mounting rails I (1" x 1" [25x25mm]) that the support rails rest on. Glue and screw the support rails on firmly.

7. Cut the housing for the legs on the large desk top in the base of the adjacent desktop. Attach the base sections to each other with clamps. Bore holes through the crossbars that lie against each other and screw together with screws and nuts.

8. Cut the desk tops.

9. Bore the holes in the corners of shelf D, which hangs under the desk. Determine where the corner brackets will be and screw them in.

10. Cut 20 pieces 7-4/5" long (20cm) of the mounting rails (1" x 1" [25x25mm]), distribute them around the desk and glue and screw them securely to the inside of the crossbars even with the top edge. Bore a hole in each. Place the MDF sheets on top and screw down well through the rails.

11. Trim the rods to the correct length, assemble them and the hanging shelf. The dome nuts are underneath.

12. Apply wood filler over all the knots. Spackle and sand. Prime twice, sand and apply one coat of enamel.

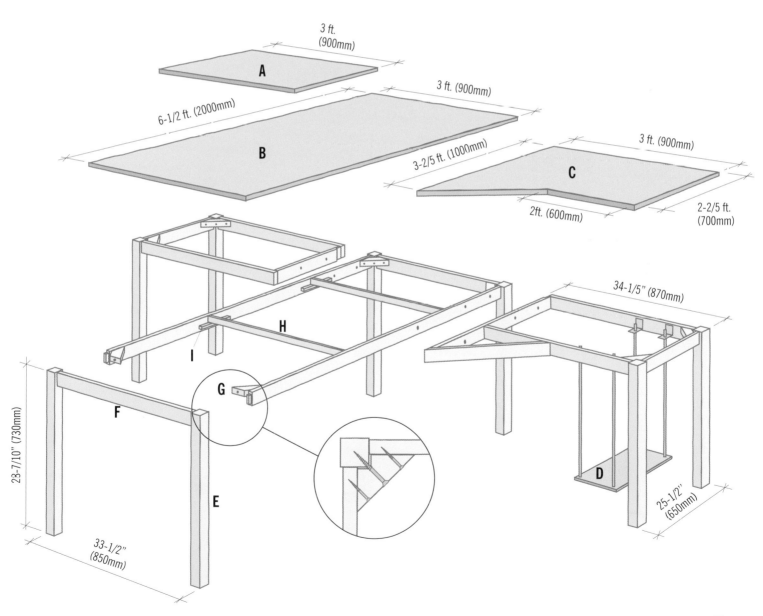

Magazine Rack

*A year's worth of magazines easily accessible.
The latest number right at the front — or maybe the one
with the prettiest cover.*

I devour magazines. It's part of my job. The piles were everywhere and it was difficult to find anything. We needed some order so why not utilize the wall?

Magazine racks are usually a bit angled so that the magazines don't fall out. This rack is straight and it depends on having every shelf full. I think that the straight rack looks better and that the shelves have come to resemble a "painting."

The magazine rack was made with milled tracks for the glass. We painted this one with red linseed oil paint to provide a contrast with all the white in our house. The rack quickly filled up and now I want more shelves just like it to hang next to it. And maybe one for the bathroom or for the cookbooks and food magazines in the kitchen?

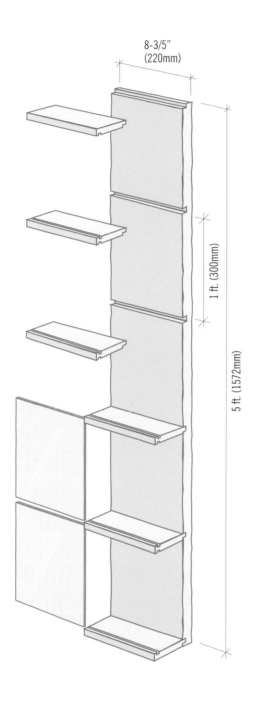

8-3/5"
(220mm)

1 ft. (300mm)

5 ft. (1572mm)

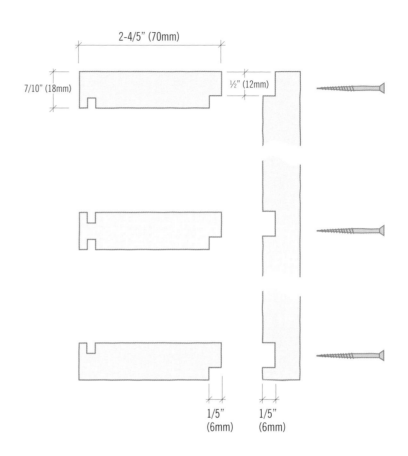

2-4/5" (70mm)

7/10" (18mm)

½" (12mm)

1/5"
(6mm)

1/5"
(6mm)

Materials

Glulam: 7/10" x 11" x 6-1/2' (18 x 300 x 2,000mm)
5 pieces glass: each 3/25" x 8-1/2" x 11" (3 x 220 x 300mm)
Glue and screws

Instructions

1. Cut the glulam down the length into two sheets with one 8-1/2" wide (220mm) and the other 2-3/4" wide (70mm).

2. Cut the wide piece for the back so that it is 62" (1,572mm).

3. Cut the narrow piece into 6 pieces, each 8-1/2" wide (220mm), for the shelves.

4. Cut 1/2" wide (12mm) dado grooves evenly spaced on the back.

5. Cut a rebate along each shelf's back edge so that they fit into the 1/2" wide (12mm) grooves.

6. Cut 3/20" deep (4mm) tracks for the glass sheets in each shelf. Use 3/20" deep (4mm) chisel steel. The top and bottom shelves only need tracks on one side.

7. Counterbore, glue and screw the shelves in from the back.

8. Measure and determine the size of the glass and then order the sheets from the glass store. It is best if you wait to order the glass until after the shelf is made because then, even if the shelves are off by a couple of mm, it won't be a disaster.

Cubbyhole for Cleaning Materials

Necessity or desire? A brilliant idea, no matter what.
The starting point for a new project can spring out of a single
impulse, but is most often a combination of several.

Our cubbyhole under the staircase, used for storing cleaning materials, was inspired by an opportunity to utilize some unused space.

As soon as I saw it, I gave myself the task of laying the tile on the floor. It was a suitable spot to first test my readiness for the art of tile-laying. It didn't need to be perfect in the cubbyhole because no one, except the family, would look in there. The result was better than expected and since then I have happily laid tiles in a number of other places.

The walls were covered with beadboard that was painted with high gloss white enamel. The door was made to fit the staircase and has the same beveled, frosted glass that shows up in many places in our home. Finally, the lion doorhandle serves a highly visible function of leading the way to the vacuum cleaner.

We have noticed that many visitors want to open the door out of curiosity, and they are clearly a little disappointed. From the outside the door and the stairs make an attractive interior decorating detail, but, from the inside — yes, a cubbyhole is a cubbyhole, even if it has a very pretty floor!

Materials

Frame: pine strips 4/5" x 2-3/4", 13ft. (22x70mm, 4m)
Bars: pine strips 4/5" x 1-4/5", 23-1/2" (22x45mm, 600mm)
Wood dowel pins 3/10" (8mm) and glue
Glass sheets: 3/20" thick (4mm) thick
Hinges (2) and magnetic lock

Instructions

1. Profile cut the rails for frame A and bar B with the router.
2. Cut the rails to the correct lengths with a miter saw, making sure that the pieces will fit the space where the door will be. The length and corners on the diagonal bar of the frame are measured after the other four parts of the frame have been cut.
3. Join the pieces with the dowel pins and glue, use webbing clamp to hold.
4. Sand, spackle, and paint.
5. Measure the size of the glass and order the sheets from the glass store.
6. Mount the glass with tacks and latex sealant.
7. Mount the hinges and magnetic lock.

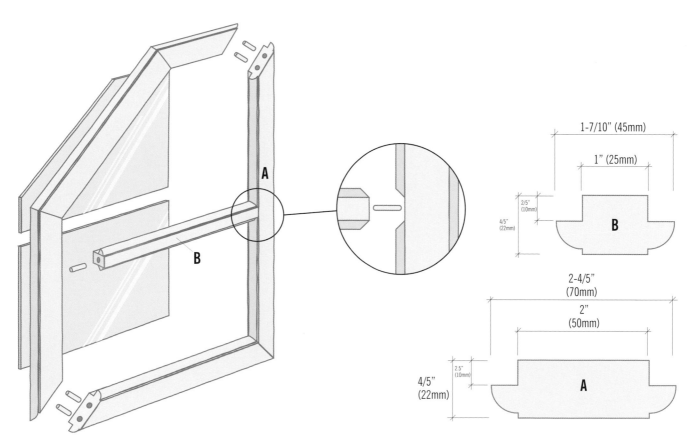

Cutting Boards

Imagine the luxury of having a cutting board just for pork fillets.

Plastic cutting boards are not nearly as nice as wood ones but sometimes they are necessary, most of all because it's easy to wash them after cutting up chicken or pork. Here's a simple little idea that popped up when we changed the bench boards in the kitchen. What can you do with scrap wood? Why not several purpose-built cutting boards?

The first result was a long, narrow cutting board that we used only for cutting pork fillets. Inspired by that, we then sketched a number of cutting boards for various purposes. We routed out small handholds on the underside.

Materials
Scrap blocks of beech wood

Instructions
1. Draw and cut the cutting boards in the shape and size you want.
2. Rout out the handholds on the underside.
3. Sand and oil until wood is saturated.

Smart hanging suggestion: A board, diagonally cut at the top, is attached to the wall and the shelf hooks onto it.

Photo Album Shelf

They usually land on the refrigerator — postcards, pictures of the children and friends, vacation shots — all held up with magnets.

That's how the idea for the album shelf came about. There was also a nostalgic aspect of the project because we don't make paper copies of photos anymore. However, we might copy some of our favorites. Old pictures or postcards from friends often bring back lovely memories and evoke a smile.

The shelf has room for eighteen albums that you stick in from the sides. Friends and relatives always stay by the shelf which is now covered with pictures to see if something new has been posted.

Materials

Front, A: MDF 1/2" x 41" x 23-1/2" (12x1050x600mm), 1 piece

Center walls, B: MDF 1/2" x 40" x 5-3/10" (12x1026x135mm), 2 pieces

Top and bottom sections, C: MDF 1/2" x 5-3/10" x 23-1/2" (12x135x600mm), 2 pieces

Shelves, D: MDF 1/2" x 5-3/10" x 10-1/2" (12x135x265mm), 4 pieces

Hanging:

E = planed wood 1-4/5" x 1-4/5" x 29-1/2" (45x45x750mm), 1 piece

F + G = planed wood 1-4/5" x 1-4/5" x 6" (45x45x150mm), 2 pieces

Short supports, H: planed rails 3/10" x 4/5" x 23-1/2" (8 x 21 x 600mm), 9 pieces

Glue, screws, threaded nails

Rods: thin, 2-3/4" long (70mm)

Instructions

Note: It is important to bore holes first before screwing into MDF sheets.

1. Screw and glue shelves D to center walls B.

2. Screw and glue the top and bottom shelves C to the center walls B. The center walls should be spaced 1-4/5" (46mm) apart.

3. Make the two blocks F and G. Cut them at a 45⁰ angle. Glue and screw the pieces together. Glue and securely screw them between the center walls B. Screw into only one of the center walls so that they aren't forced together.

4. Attach the small rails to front A with glue and a few small nails.

5. Cut grooves in rails H, 3/20" (4mm) in the rail width and 3/25" (3mm) in the thickness. The top and bottom rails should be cut on one side only.

6. Attached the rails with glue and a few small nails. It is important to space them precisely equidistant.

7. Cut a 45⁰ angle at one end of each board E (29-1/2" long or 750mm). Bore a hole in it and attach to the wall using a level to make sure it is straight.

8. Hang the shelf on the board.

9. Bore a hole through the center walls B and board E on the lowest partition. Insert a 2-3/4" long (70mm) rod through the hole to attach the shelf.

10. Cover any knots with wood filler. Spackle and sand. Prime twice, sand, and coat with enamel.

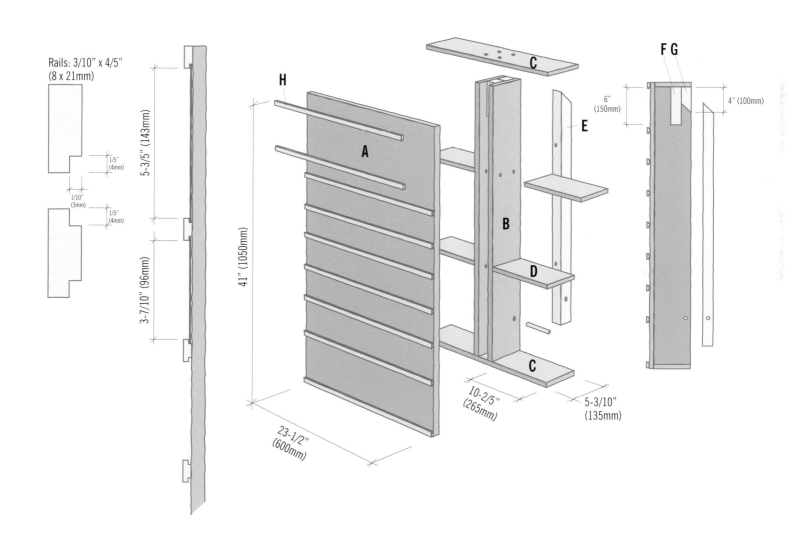

Music Shelf

An open and tidy music shelf — the supports are at the right height and there is room for all the CDs we are playing the most right now.

The music shelf is made with beech. A couple of narrow strips on the back keep the shelf a few inches/centimeters from the wall and allow the heavy construction to float a little more freely. The glass shelf adds to the floating impression. The cords — a perpetual and unavoidable tangle — are not a problem as we've spirited them away in a storage space on the back.

Maybe there isn't so much rock 'n roll above the shelf but sweet music arises when the vacuum cleaner never has to squeeze in between the legs. The wall hanging is almost always a hit!

Materials

Planed beech: 1-2/5" x 1/2" (35x15mm): A. 2 pieces, 16" (405mm) ea., B. 2 pieces, 21-1/2" (550mm) ea., E. 2 pieces, 19" (480mm) ea.

Planed beech: 2-3/4" x 1/2" (70x15mm): C. 2 pieces, 53-1/2" (1360mm) ea., D. 1 piece, 17-1/2" (450mm), F. 1 piece, 17-1/2" (450mm)

Frosted glass, 3/20" (4mm): 1 sheet, 18" x 17" (458x440mm); 3 pieces, 18" x 5-7/10" (458x145mm)

10 wood plugs

1 magnet lock

2 hinges

Glue and wood dowel pins

Instructions

1. Cut and join braces A and B with wood dowel pins and glue. The angle between the pieces should be approx 49°. Cut the top piece (A) first, after assembly, so that it is easier to get the correct length and angle on it.

2. Cut the long sides C and then cut 2/10" deep (5mm) grooves for the glass sheets with a router. Clamp with a board to keep straight.

3. Join shelf D with two wood dowel pins in each end.

4. Screw in the top crossbar E firmly.

5. Join the braces (A + B) with wood dowel pins and glue against the long sides C. Place part A exactly along the bottom edge of the groove for the glass sheet.

6. Screw the lower crossbar E in firmly. If the braces haven't been cut at exactly the correct angle, this bar can end up a little higher or lower.

7. Cut flap F and attach it with a hinge into shelf D.

8. Mount the magnet lock.

9. Bore holes in the top crossbar E for the wall mounting.

10. Set up the music shelf on the wall and slide the glass plate into place.

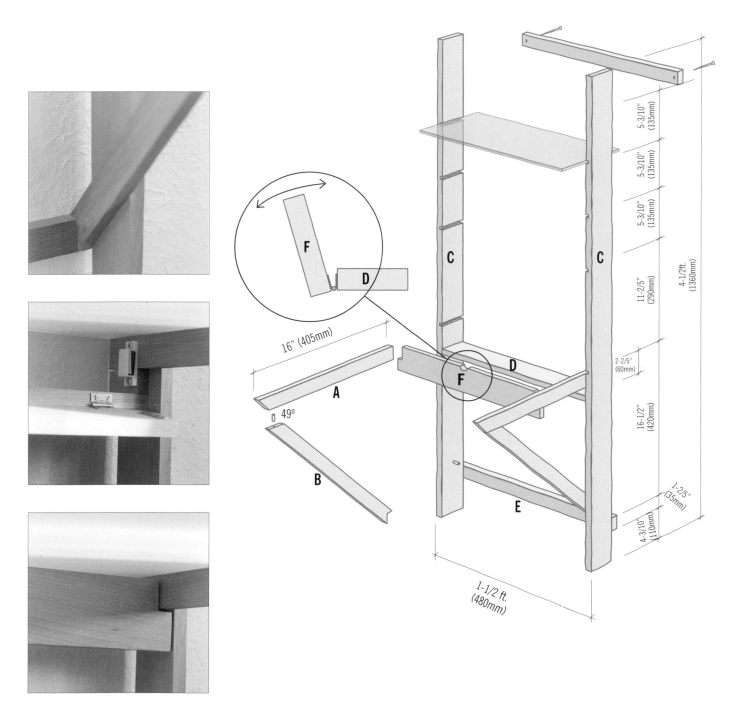

Mailbox

We really needed a new mailbox. The old one, besides looking very scruffy, couldn't hold a great deal of mail. We had to go to the post office to pick up the large-size envelopes that wouldn't fit.

The new box, with its two-shelf structure, is wonderful. When we travel, we can remove the top "floor" (shelf) and then the box has space for a whole week's worth of mail. We can lock the side door for removing the mail with a padlock before the trip, but the sliding lock is good enough for everyday use.

As an alternative to building a base for the mailbox, we chose to anchor it to the fence instead. The roof was made with wood strips and regular roofing felt so that it would be perfectly rounded and give the box some character. A simple trick was to hang a block as a weight on the inside of the door so that it would shut as the mail carrier went on his/her way. The box itself is made with water-resistant plywood and painted white to match the fence. We'll see how long it stays white, though. If it doesn't, we'll paint it green like the hedge.

Materials

Plywood, 7/25" thick (7mm):

    A. 2 pieces, 48" x 15-1/2" (1240x400mm)

    B. 2 pieces, 45-1/2" x 11-4/5" (1160x300mm)

    C. 2 pieces, 15" x 11" (385x285mm)

    D. 1 piece, 12-1/2" x 9-1/2" (320x240mm)

    E. 1 piece, 11-4/5" x 4-710" (300x120mm)

    F. 1 piece, 15" x 6" (385x150mm)

Planed wood:

    3/5" x 3/5", 11 yds. (16x16mm, 10m)

    3/5" x 1-4/5", 4-1/2 yds. (16x45mm, 4.2m)

    4/5" x 3-7/10, 1 yd. (22x95mm, 900mm)

    4/5" x 2-3/4", 2-1/2 ft. (22x70mm, 800mm)

Dimensional lumber: 1-4/5" x 2-3/4", 1 ft. (45x70mm, 320mm)

Slip molding: 3/10" x 4/5", 2 ft. (8x21mm, 600mm)

2 piano hinges

Sliding bolt

Roofing felt

Glue and screws

Instructions

1. Cut the plywood pieces.

2. Cut the rails G (3/5" x 3/5" [16x16mm]). Glue and firmly screw them in 7/25" (7mm) from the edge on one side of the front and back pieces A. Counterbore holes into the plywood.

3. Glue and screw rails H firmly to the bottom shelves C on the front and back pieces A and the side pieces B, the rails H to shelf F on the side pieces B as well as the rails in the flap opening on one side piece B (a total of 3/5" x 3/5" [16x16mm]). Note that the rail on the hinge side of the emptying flap D sits edge to edge with the plywood while the other rail makes a stop for the flap and therefore sits a bit into the opening.

4. Cut the two swinging pieces J (4/5" x 2-3/4" [22x70mm]); glue and screw them firmly on the inside of the front and back pieces A. Later you will screw the roof onto these pieces.

5. Crosscut the two drip rails K and L (4/5" x 2-3/4" [16x45mm]); glue and screw them in over the hole for the flaps.

6. Glue and screw the board piece M on the inside of the mail slot flap. Glue/nail the slip molding N (3/10 x 4/5" [8x21mm]) on the flap's outside so it won't stick underneath the plywood.

7. Glue and firmly screw on rail O (3/5" x 3/5" [16x16mm]), that the hinge will be attached to, on the inside of the emptying flap D and glue/nail slip molding P on the lower edge of this outside.

8. Attach both flaps with the piano hinges.

9. Glue and screw the four front, back, and side pieces A and B together. Glue and screw shelf F in firmly.

10. Cut boards Q (3/5" x 1-4/5" [16x45mm]) for the roof. Glue and screw them into place.

11. Cut the roofing felt and nail it well to the roof with tacks along the lower edge.

12. Cut the curved attic pieces R from the board that is 4/5" x 3-1/2" (22x90mm). Glue and screw them on securely.

13. Now it's time to work on the outside of the mailbox. Tighten all the gaps with latex sealant. Coat all the wood ends with wood filler. Apply two coats of primer, sand lightly, and apply one coat of enamel.

14. Mount the mailbox on the fence or whatever it will sit on with carriage bolts. Finally, slide in the bottom shelves C.

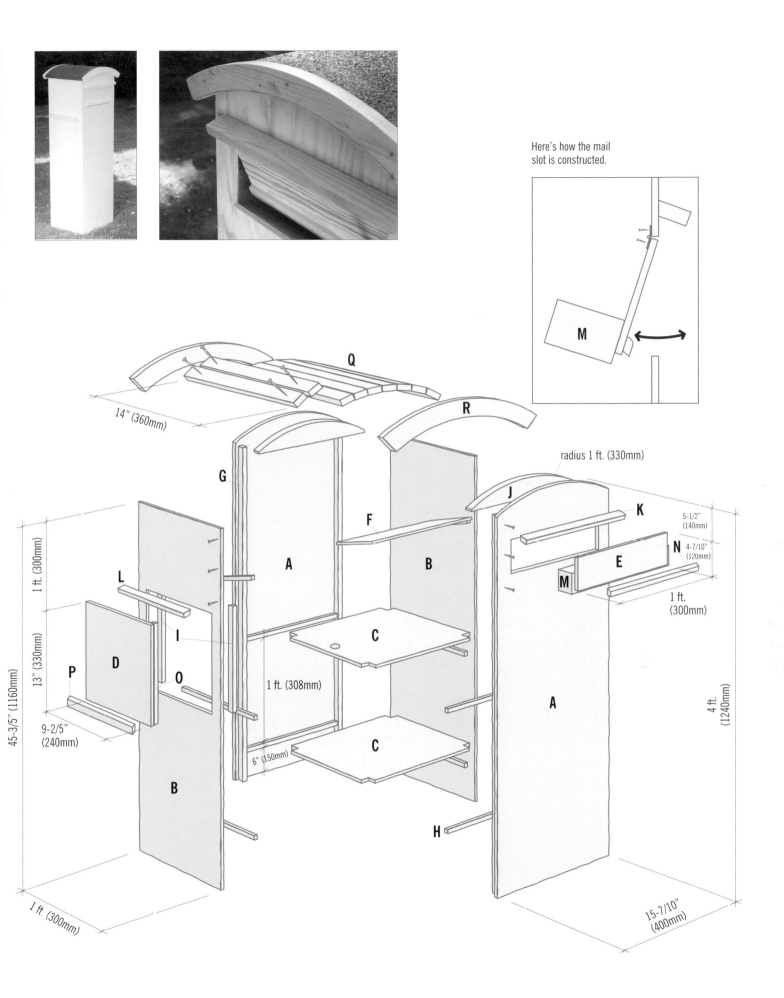

Here's how the mail slot is constructed.

14" (360mm)

radius 1 ft. (330mm)

5-1/2" (140mm)

4-7/10" (120mm)

1 ft. (300mm)

1 ft. (300mm)

1 ft. (308mm)

6" (150mm)

9-2/5" (240mm)

13" (330mm)

45-3/5" (1160mm)

1 ft. (300mm)

4 ft. (1240mm)

15-7/10" (400mm)

Q
R
G
F
A
B
J
K
N
E
M
L
I
D
O
P
C
C
B
A
H

Plant Stand

*Spring. Anticipation. I'm getting impatient —
must help spring get moving.*

Often and much too early, I sow too many seeds in quite a few pots. A while ago we moved the table forward so that the window wouldn't be too tightly packed — that proved to be unwieldy and, if truth be told, not particularly pretty. It became one big mess of seedlings.

What we needed was a shelf that could easily fold down for storage when all the plants were put out in the garden beds...a shelf with space for lots of pots.

Our flower shelf had several more functions than I originally imagined possible. In the summer, it goes out onto the terrace where it can be filled with plants. In the fall it goes down to the basement. Yes, we could also mention that it might even move into the kitchen to hold the potted herbs.

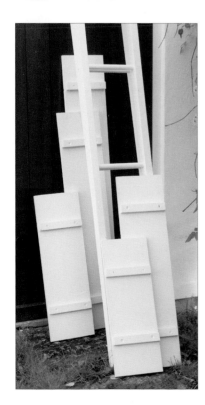

Instructions

1. Cut the four legs A and the rods D.

2. Bore 4/5" deep (20mm) holes for the rods in the legs. Assemble and glue the two "steps" together. Screw in the screws through the legs and in the end wood of the poles.

3. Lay both "steps" on the floor with the tops facing each other — make sure that they lie straight — and screw in the hinges.

4. Cut the boards for the shelves B. Each shelf consists of two boards. If necessary or desired, add 3/8" or more extra.

5. Screw and firmly glue on the shelf supports to the lower shelf, spaced well enough apart. Test the spacing by pulling the legs apart to the right distance and then slide the shelf in. Mark the placement of the rails on the underside of the shelf.

6. Set the other shelf into place, test and measure as for the first shelf.

7. Put the shelves into place, mark for cutting, and then cut.

Materials

Planed wood:

A. 4 legs 1-3/10" x 1-4/5", 6-1/2 ft. (34 x 45mm, 2050mm)

B. shelves 4/5" x 3-7/10", 8-1/2" yds. (22 x 95mm, approx. 8m)

C. 10 shelf rails 4/5" x 1-4/5", 7-1/2" (22 x 45mm, 190mm)

D. 10 rods, 1", 9-4/5" (25mm diameter, 250mm)

2 hinges

Screws

Glue

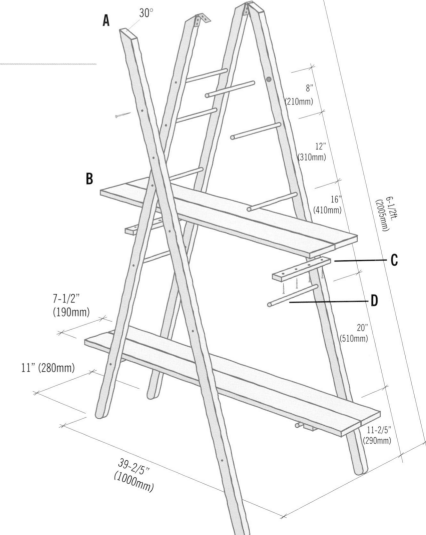

Cookbook Stand

Big, little, thick, thin. It doesn't matter what the cookbooks look like for this flexible cookbook stand. The plexiglass sheets can be moved and placed to fit the book being used. The base is made of oak with several grooves cut into it and the sheets are cut from plexiglass. Simple, somewhat subdued, and no more messy cookbooks.

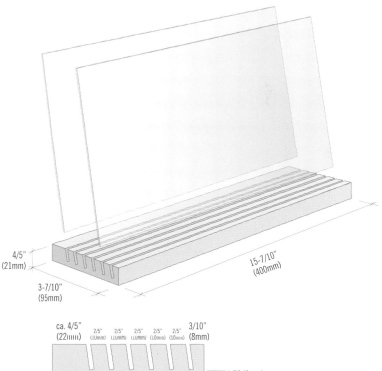

Materials
Planed oak: 4/5" x 3-7/10", 15-1/2" (21x95mm, 400mm)
Plexiglass: 2 sheets each 2/5" x 10-1/2" x 15-1/2" (2x270x400mm)

Instructions
1. Set the circular saw at an approx. 9º angle and 3/5" deep (15mm) deep.
2. Cut 6 incisions in the oak board.
3. Sand and oil the wood to a fine finish.
4. Set in the sheets of plexiglass.

Note Boxes

The boxes are a bit reminiscent of a magazine rack. They're perfect for collecting the children's papers from school, their keys, and the cell phones.

When the chaos caused by all the papers from school and information from different activities got too much and when Ida became irritated every morning trying to find her keys, the idea for the note boxes was born. Now each girl has her own.

Each box consists of three compartments with Plexiglas walls in between, and recesses, so even little papers can be found. We based the back with "magnet" paint at the top so that messages and to-do lists could be hung up with magnets. The note boxes function well and I wonder if I should ask Anders to make one for me also. Guess who is irritated now looking for her keys and cell phone?

Instructions

1. Cut the pieces of MDF.

2. Cut 3/30" wide (4mm) and 3/25" deep (3mm) grooves for the Plexiglass in the side pieces. End the grooves 2/5" (10mm) from the lower edge.

3. Mark where each biscuit should be placed and cut the grooves for them with a "biscuit cutter." Note that the back and front pieces will stick out laterally from the sides when the pieces are assembled.

4. Join the side pieces and bottom with biscuits and glue. Clamp and let dry.

5. Attach the front and back pieces the same way to the sides and bottom. Clamp and let dry.

6. Bore holes in the back for the hanging hooks.

7. Cut notch in the Plexiglas with a figure saw.

8. Attach the hooks and slide the Plexiglas into place.

9. Apply several coats of "magnet paint" on the back before priming and painting the box.

Materials

MDF sheets, 7/20" thick (9mm):
A. 1 piece 17-1/2" x 9-1/2" (450x240mm)
B. 2 pieces each 11-4/5" x 7" (300x180mm)
C. 1 piece 2-3/4" x 9-1/2" (70x240mm)
MDF sheet, 3/5" thick (16mm):
D. 1 piece 8-1/2" x 7" (215x180mm)
Plexiglas, 3/25" thick (3mm);
E. 1 piece 8-1/2" x 9-1/4" (220x235mm)
F. 1 piece 8-1/2" x 6-9/10" (220x175mm)
Wood biscuits (8) and wood glue
2 coat hooks

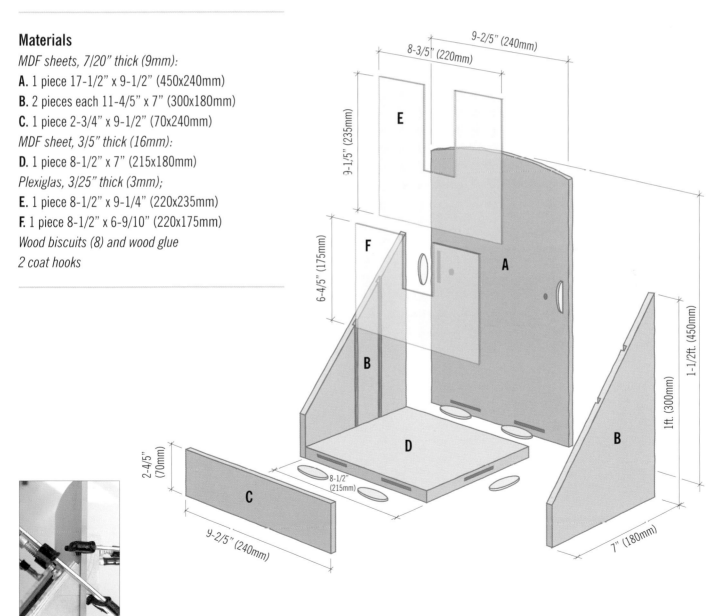

119

Pantry

I've always dreamt of a large kitchen with a walk-in pantry with plain shelves so that I can easily find everything I'm looking for.

Our kitchen didn't have enough room for the pantry of my dreams, but we made another version that works just as well. The sense of a large country pantry is fantastic.

When we moved into our house, we discovered a small, bricked-up window behind the refrigerator. We moved the refrigerator, moved the window out, and put the pantry there.

We made the pantry with traditional beadboard and painted it with high gloss enamel, which is pretty on woodwork and practical in a kitchen. The shelves rest on brackets made with 1" (25mm) squared rails as in traditional designs. The door is perpendicular to a side wall, which means that the pantry doesn't take up much more room than a regular cupboard but clearly appears larger. The window is, of course, one of the reasons for that.

The door is perpendicular to a side wall. The cat, Amanda, looks like she is about to take a nap in the beautiful spring sunshine.

The space between the pantry and the ceiling is covered by a molding. All the cracks are filled with latex sealant. Grandmother's old clock from the 1950s has a fine, central place.

Materials

Planed wood: 4/5" x 1-4/5", 36 yds. (22x45mm, approx. 33m)

18 pieces beadboard: 1/2" x 3-7/10", 3 yds. (12x95mm, 2.7m)

Molding: country style 3/5" x 2-3/10", 1-1/2 yds. (15x59mm, 1.5m)

S4S planed rail supports: 7/20" x 2/25", 2yds. (9x2mm, 2m)

Hinges and hasp

Nails

Screws

Glue

Basic shelves!
The panty isn't always so empty, but, even when it is full, I don't have to root around to find something. In addition, I don't have to throw out old food. Another practical little necessity taken care of.

Instructions

Adjust measurements to your space. Build the wood frame in situ, screwing the pieces together.

1. Cut the boards that will face the walls, firmly screw the crossbars into the wall boards before screwing them to the wall.

2. Screw in the top and bottom crossbars to the ceiling and floor.

3. Cut the four corner boards at an angle. Measure out the angles in place.

4. Firmly screw the first corner board on each side of the four crossbars.

5. Glue and screw in the two remaining corner boards.

6. Cut and screw in the two crossbars above the door.

7. Attach a thin rail (7/20" x 4/5" [9x22mm]) in the inside of the door opening so that it prevents the door from opening inward.

8. Cut and screw together the door frame, making it a few millimeters smaller than the door opening. Assemble the frame in place with the hinges, which should stick out to the same measurement as the thickness of the beadboard.

9. Cut and firmly screw in the diagonal bars in the door so that the door is angled correctly.

10. Cut and screw the crossbars firmly to the door.

11. Clad the whole frame and the door with beadboard. Apply a fine coat of glue and carefully nail in the grooves. The glue is particularly important for the door.

12. Cut and attach the molding to the ceiling. Use wood filler to cover any knots. Apply latex sealant to all the cracks. Apply two coats of primer. Sand and apply one coat of enamel.

13. Mount the hasp.

14. Build basic shelving for the pantry.

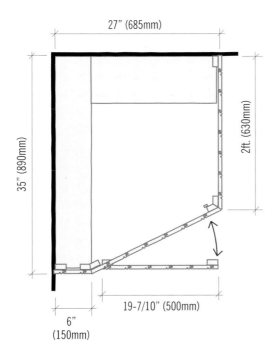

27" (685mm)

35" (890mm)

2ft. (630mm)

19-7/10" (500mm)

6" (150mm)

124

Play Station

Climb, swing, balance, and maybe even sail:
Our play station has several functions where creativity determines the game.

The play station is stable and sturdy enough so that even adults can try it out, which the children sometimes insist on. Another advantage is that many children can play on it at the same time. Hilda's sixth birthday party set the record — 18 children on the station!

We call the play station "Wild Hilda" after that daughter. At first it seems like it will take some time to make, but the construction is easy and the project moves along much more quickly than you'd think.

The planks are both a swing and a balance board. As for the steps — or is it a mast? — you can hold onto them when the game is at its wildest or climb up to the top for scouting the territory better. Only one's imagination sets the boundaries!

One person can easily move the play station by pulling it. And Wild Hilda can sail to whatever part of the yard seems best. That also benefits the lawn.

Ida and Hilda, along with their friend, Daniel, take a car — or a sailing — trip. Or maybe just a regular swing.

Materials

Pressure-treated wood: 1-4/5" x 5-1/2" (45x145mm)

    A. 1 piece 12-1/2 ft. (3,880mm)

    B. 2 pieces each 1/2 ft. (150mm)

    C. 1 piece 9 ft. (570mm)

    E. 2 pieces each: 1-1/2 ft. (450mm), 1-4/5" x 2-3/4" (45x70mm)

    D. 2 pieces each: 5-1/2 ft. (1,720mm), 1-4/5" x 1-4/5" (45x45mm)

    F. 4 pieces each: 6 ft. (1,830mm), 4/5" x 4" (21x105mm)

    G. 4 pieces, each 2-1/2 ft. (800mm)

7 pieces rods: 4/5" diameter, 1-3/10" (21mm diameter, 400mm)

French wood screws with washers:

    9 pieces: 3/10" x 4-1/2" (8x120mm)

    12 pieces: 3/10" x 3/4" (8x75mm)

24 screws: 4/25" x 3/4" (4.3x75mm)

Rope: 11 yds. (10 m)

Instructions

1. Screw B pieces firmly into board A.

2. Attach the long board A in the strong upright board C with a strong French wood screw. Make sure pieces are centered.

3. Screw in side boards D.

4. Cut the two curved pieces E and screw them in securely.

5. Screw on the diagonals F, first at the bottom and then at the top. Do not bore holes for the screws in board A because this is now your chance to pull the construction to the correct angles. Bore and screw.

6. Screw boards G to the underside of E with a number of long and sturdy screws because there is a lot of stress here.

7. Bore the holes for the rods H and press them into place, secure with screws.

8. Bore holes for the rope and attach it.

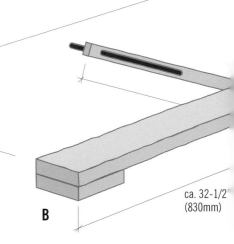

ca. 32-1/2"
(830mm)

B

If you want a flag, you don't have to make it yourself. You can find them in toy stores.

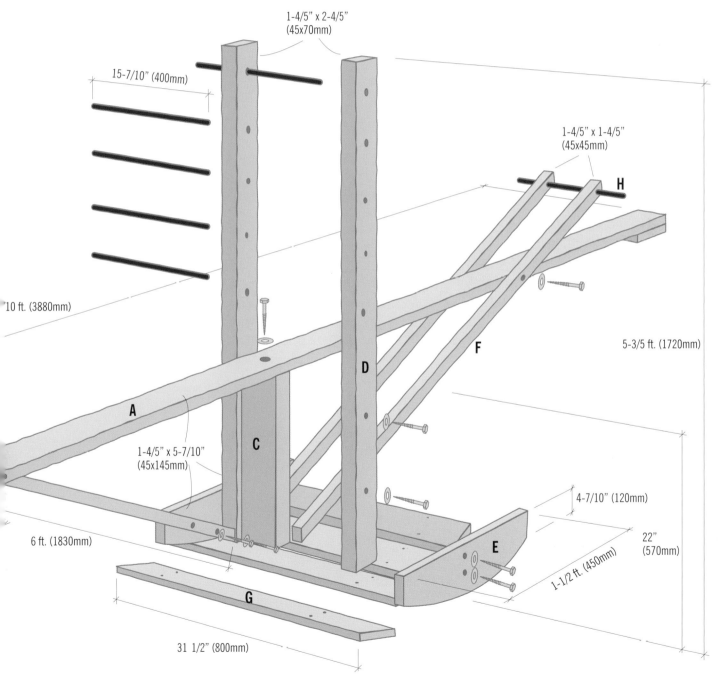

1-4/5" x 2-4/5"
(45x70mm)

15-7/10" (400mm)

1-4/5" x 1-4/5"
(45x45mm)

H

10 ft. (3880mm)

5-3/5 ft. (1720mm)

F

A

D

1-4/5" x 5-7/10"
(45x145mm)

C

4-7/10" (120mm)

6 ft. (1830mm)

E

22"
(570mm)

1-1/2 ft. (450mm)

G

31 1/2" (800mm)

Garden Furniture

Our terrace faces south and is well-protected from the cold wind. The first rays of sun warm it up very early in the spring.

Traditionally, we invite our closest friends over on Good Friday for a "herring lunch." For the past few years, we've been lucky with the weather. We set the large table, and the Easter herring, potatoes, and accompanying schnapps can be enjoyed on the terrace.

The benches were sketched first without the back supports, but, since we sometimes sit at the table for a long time, back support became necessary. For a long time, I went to flea markets looking for classic park benches but without success.

Inspired by the park bench style and its usually simple design, we designed and built our own garden furniture.

Table

Materials

Dimensional lumber:
1-4/5" x 5-1/2", 2-1/2 yds. (45x145mm, 2.4m)
1-4/5" x 3-7/10", 3 yds. (45x95mm, 2.8m)
1-4/5" x 2-3/4" 1-3/4 yds. (45x70mm, 1.6m)
1-4/5" x 1-4/5", 8 yds. (45x45mm, 7.5m)
Planed wood:
4/5" x 3-7/10", 18-1/2 yds. (22x95mm, 17m)
Rods: 1/2" diameter, 15-1/2" (12mm diameter, 400mm)
6 hinges (strong)
Wood glue
Wood dowel pins
Screws

Instructions

1. Cut the parts for the frame pieces A-D (1-4/5" x 1-4/5" [45x45mm]) for the table top. Bore holes for the oblique bars I in the center parts D with a 3/5" (15mm) bore before placing the parts together. The distance between the holes should be 12-2/5" (315mm). Glue and screw the pieces together.
2. Cut the 4 legs E (1-4/5" x 5-3/10 [45x145mm]), 23-1/2" long (600mm).
3. Cut the 2 crossbars F (1-4/5" x 3-7/10" [45x95mm]), 11-2/5" long (290mm). Cut and chisel out a 1-4/5" wide (45mm) notch for the crossbar's half height.
4. Join the legs E and the crossbars F with wood dowel pins and glue. Clamp and let dry.

The table can be folded flat and stored for the winter without taking up a lot of space.

5. Draw and cut the feet G (1-4/5" x 2-3/4" [45x70mm]). Glue and screw securely to legs E.
6. Join legs E and frame boards B with hinges.
7. Cut the support boards H (1-4/5" x 3-7/10" [45x95mm]) between the pairs of legs. Set up the table, straight and perpendicular, measure and mark on board H where the notch should be. Cut and chisel out a 1-4/5" wide (45mm) notch for the board's half height at the markings.
8. Cut the oblique bars I (1-4/5" x 1-4/5" [45x45mm]), 31-1/2" long (800mm). Mount them with hinges on support board H.
9. Place the support board H in the notch in crossbars F, lift up the oblique bars I and mark placement of the holes in them. Bore the holes and cut 2 rods each 7-4/5" (200mm) and assemble table.
10. Draw and cut off the part of the oblique bars I that stick out above frame A-D.
11. Cut the boards J (4/5" x 3-7/10" [22x95mm]) for the table top 9 ft. long (2,400mm). Glue and screw firmly into the frame.

Finishing

Oil all the parts, particularly the exposed wood ends of the boards, and let dry. Apply two coats of primer; sand lightly and apply one coat of enamel for outdoor use.

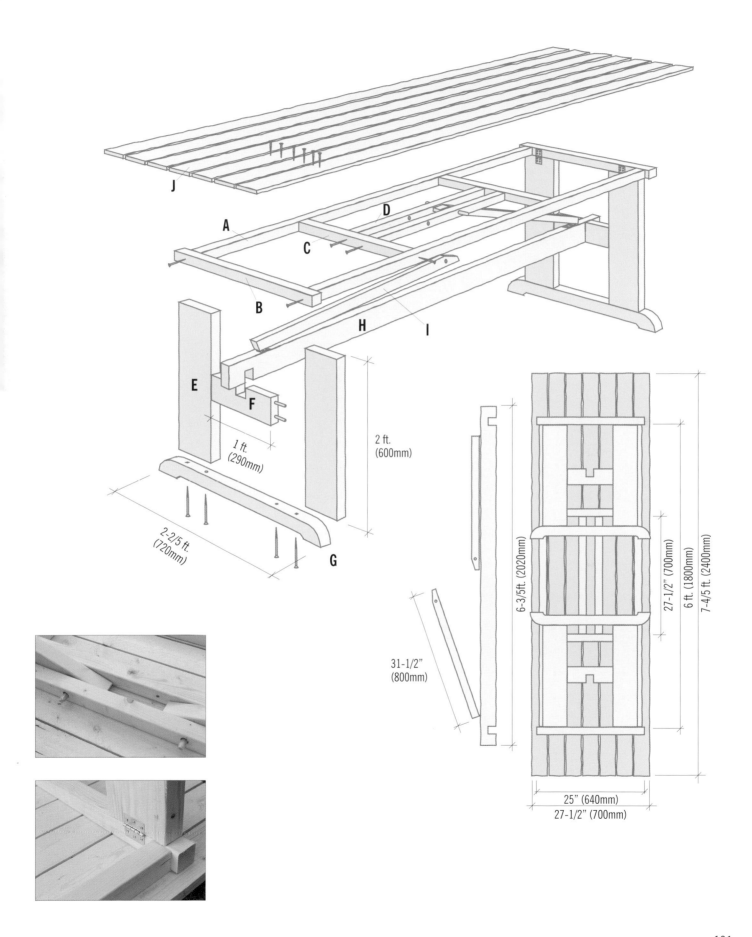

A

J

D

C

B

H

I

E

F

G

1 ft.
(290mm)

2 ft.
(600mm)

2-2/5 ft.
(720mm)

31-1/2"
(800mm)

6-3/5 ft. (2020mm)

27-1/2" (700mm)

6 ft. (1800mm)

7-4/5 ft. (2400mm)

25" (640mm)

27-1/2" (700mm)

Bench

Materials for one bench

Dimesional wood:
1-4/5" x 5-7/10", 6-1/2 yds. (45x145mm, 6m)
1-4/5" x 2-3/4", 1 yd. (45x70mm, 1m)
1-4/5" x 1-4/5", 4-1/2 yds. (45x45mm, 4.2m)
Planed wood: 4/5" x 3-7/10, 13 ft. (22x95mm, 4m)
Rods: 1/2" diameter, 1 yd. (12mm diameter, 1m)
6 hinges (strong)
Wood glue
Screws

Instructions

1. Cut 2 pieces of lumber each 6-1/2 ft. long (2m) for the seat A and 4 pieces each 13-1/2" (345mm) for the legs B (a total of 1-4/5" x 5-7/10" [45x145mm]).

2. Cut 2 boards C (1-4/5" x 1-4/5" [45x45mm]) so that they are 14" long (355mm). Bore a 1/2" (15mm) hole a little bit in from one end. Screw and glue boards C firmly to boards A for the seat following the illustration.

3. Plane or cut off the rounded ends on one side of the four short pieces for legs B and glue them together in pairs. Clamp and let dry.

4. Draw and cut the feet D (1-4/5" x 2-3/4" [45x70mm]). Glue and screw in firmly to legs B.

5. Assemble legs B with the hinges on the underside of the seat.

6. Cut 2 pieces each 25-1/2" (650mm) for the braces F (1-4/5" x 1-4/5" [45x45mm]). Try them out and then cut the angles on the bottom of each brace. Attach the braces with hinges in the leg (temporarily at first in case you need to remove it to cut and bore). Check and then cut the angles at the other end of the braces.

7. Cut out 4 blocks E (1-4/5" x 1-4/5" [45x45mm]) that are 4-7/10" long (12cm). Bore a 1/2" (15mm) hole in each of the blocks and glue and screw them onto the underside of the seat.

8. Make sure that the bench stands straight and that the legs are at the correct angle; mark positions and bore 1/2" (15mm) holes in braces F.

9. Cut 2 rods and assemble the bench.

10. Cut 2 pieces each 23-1/2" (600mm) for the back supports G (1-4/5" x 1-4/5" [45x45mm]). Hold them against the bench at the desired angle, draw, and cut.

11. Cut 2 back boards H (4/5" x 3-7/10" [22x95mm]) each 6-1/2 ft. long (2m). Glue and screw the parts of the back together.

12. Holding the back in place, mark placement for screw holes in the back supports and bore.

13. Cut 2 rods and assemble the back.

Finishing

Finish the bench as for the table.

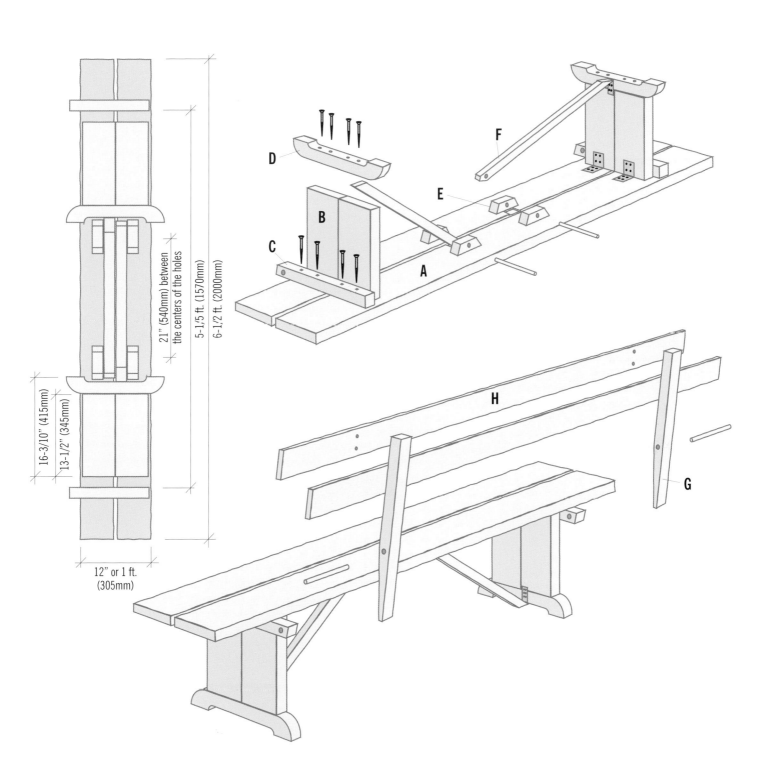

21" (540mm) between the centers of the holes

5-1/5 ft. (1570mm)

6-1/2 ft. (2000mm)

16-3/10" (415mm)

13-1/2" (345mm)

12" or 1 ft. (305mm)

A

B

C

D

E

F

G

H

Bowl Holder

Olives, marinated garlic, sun-dried tomatoes ... Why not a variety of jams for breakfast? It's your choice, and how nice they look, each in their own bowl.

Each bowl sits sturdily in its hole in the bowl holder.

Two boards, in this case oak, and a hole-cutter in the drill — big enough for the bowls you've selected — is all you need.

Bore three holes in one board, glue the boards together and finish with fine sandpaper. It's a simple idea, but often it's the small details that make the difference when setting the table.

Materials

Planed oak: 4/5" x 3-7/10", 27-1/2" (22x95mm, 700mm)
Wood glue

Instructions

1. Cut the oak boards into 2 pieces.
2. Outline the holes on one board and cut the hole with a hole saw to desired size.
3. Glue the pieces together, clamp and let dry.
4. Cut the holder to the desired length at both ends.
5. Sand lightly and oil finish.

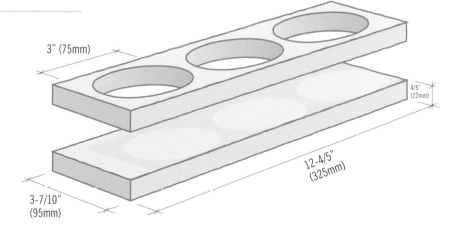

3" (75mm)

4/5" (22mm)

12-4/5" (325mm)

3-7/10" (95mm)

Bathroom Cabinet and Shelf

The bathroom was a disaster when we moved in.
We had to totally remodel, removing the gray linoleum that was on the walls
and floor. We renovated in a style that we thought suited the house.

The tile selection, the French balcony with its frosted glass doors, and the cast iron bathtub determined the look of the shelf and the cabinet.

It was a simple cabinet sized to fit the bathroom wall. The door and shelves are just frosted glass. We screwed in metal clothes hooks on the bottom of the cabinet. Then we made a shelf to fit on another wall in the same bathroom, using the same type of hook for the towels. The supports on the back run in one piece behind both shelves. The shelves are beveled on one side because we wanted to avoid sharp corners at head height.

When the doors to the French balcony are closed in the evening, the frosted glass provides privacy. Otherwise the doors are open weather permitting.

Cabinet

Materials

Planed wood:
3/5" x 5-7/10", 6-1/2 ft. (16x145mm, 2m)
4/5" x 3/5", 6-1/2 ft. (22x16mm, 2m)
Masonite: 18-2/5 x 18-2/5" (467x467mm)
Crude glass: 3/25" (3mm); 1 piece 19" x 19" (480x480mm)
and 2 pieces each 18-2/5" x 5-1/2" (467x140mm)
Hinges (2) and magnetic lock
Wood glue, wood biscuits, and threaded nails
Latex sealant

Instructions

1. Cut the 2 pieces for the sides each 19-1/2" (500mm) and a top and bottom piece each 1-1/2 ft. (468mm) for the cabinet (3/5" x 5-7/10" [16x145mm]).

2. Cut a groove in the cabinet pieces for the masonite for the back. Avoid cutting up to the ends of the side pieces.

3. Cut 1/5" deep (5mm) grooves for the glass for the shelves in the side pieces.

4. Mill out the housing for the biscuits in the side, top and bottom pieces. Join the cabinet pieces with glue and biscuits. Clamp and let dry.

5. Glue and nail the masonite sheet on the back of the cabinet.

6. Cut out a track for the glass in the rails (4/5" x 3/5" [22x16mm]) for the door.

7. Miter cut the rails, glue and nail together into a frame.

8. Put the glass into the frame and secure with small tacks and latex sealant.

9. Countersink for the hinges in one side piece. Mount the door with the hinges.

10. Bore a hole for the small magnetic lock and mount it.

11. Bore a hole at each top corner of the masonite sheet so that the cabinet can be hung on the wall. Use large washers for setting up.

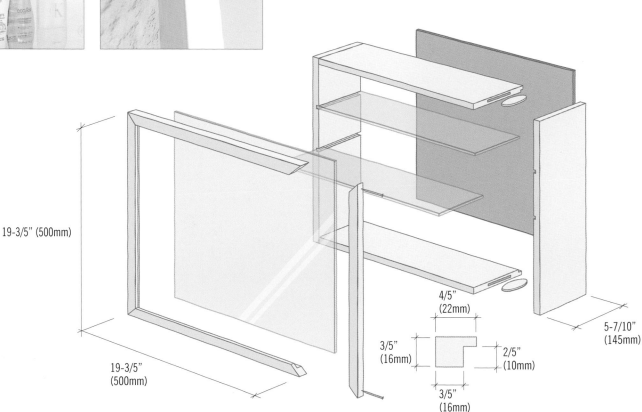

19-3/5" (500mm)

19-3/5" (500mm)

4/5" (22mm)

3/5" (16mm)

2/5" (10mm)

3/5" (16mm)

5-7/10" (145mm)

Shelf

Materials

Tongue-and-groove boards: 4/5" x 3-7/10", 29-1/2 ft. (21x95mm, 9m)
Planed rails: 3/5" x 1-1/10", 11-1/2 ft. [16x28mm, 3.5m])
Wood glue
Screws

Instructions

1. Cut the tongue-and-groove boards into 8 pieces each 3-1/2 ft. (1100mm) and glue together 4 by 4. Clamp and let dry.

2. Cut out the shelves and profile cut along the edge. Cut and chisel out the notches for the braces on the back edge.

3. Cut out the pieces for the braces. Begin with the vertical ones and then the horizontals. Cut and chisel the notches for the horizontals in the vertical pieces. Put the pieces into place at the correct angle. Lay the oblique piece on top at a 45° angle, and mark how the pieces should be cut.

4. Bore holes for the screws needed to assemble. Glue and screw the braces together.

5. Glue the shelf onto the braces.

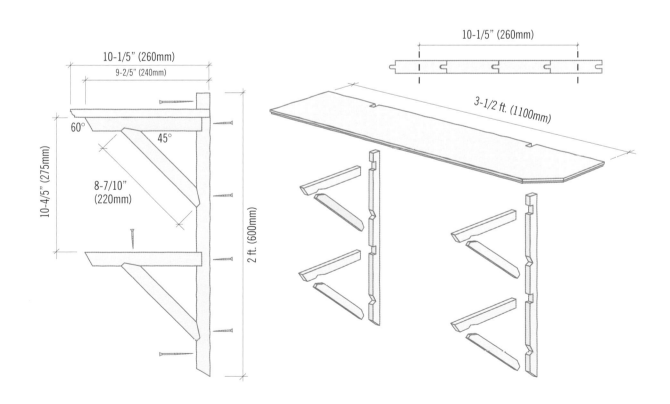

Bed Frame

*When we travel around in the English countryside and stay at
country houses, pubs or bed and breakfasts
my constant question is:
"Is it possible to get a room with a four-poster bed?"
The answer is most often "yes!"*

We've taken some fantastic trips to England. We've rented a car and driven around without a particular destination in mind. We've found some small towns and villages with, what seemed to us, the absolutely finest architecture. We've met wonderful people in the local pubs and visited garden centers and castles with greenhouses that we'd only previously seen in pictures.

Every night in a new hotel room and my question was always the same: "Do you have a room with a four-poster bed?"

None of the beds have been exactly like the others: some are large, a little overblown with thick, elaborate posts while others are a little more slender but with the same inviting feeling.

So simple and at the same time effective...a bed with four posts. That's what it's about. Because you can choose the crosspieces, thickness, color and fabric, the possibilities for variation are endless.

We built a rather simple bed for our guests with a small moveable night table. It is olive green with fine white curtains and Indian lanterns. We used Anders' oil painting of a woman as a headboard. And if any of our guests, contrary to expectations, choose to get up early, I'll get up and begin serving scrambled eggs, toast, and English breakfast tea!

Bed

Materials

Planed wood

A + B: 8 ea. 4/5" x 3-7/10" (22x95mm), 6-1/2 ft. (2000mm)

C + I: 1-4/5" x 1-4/5" (45x45mm); 4 ea. 9" (230mm);
2 ea. 6 ft. (1800mm)

D: 4 ea. 3/5" x 3/5" (16x16mm), 4" (100mm)

E + F: 4/5" x 1-3/10" (22x34mm); 2 ea. 4 ft. (1247mm);
2 ea. 6-1/2" (2043mm)

J + K: 2 ea. 1 yd. (1000mm); 4 ea. 4" (100mm)

Glulam sheet

G+H: 4/5" x 7-4/5" (20x200mm); 2 ea. 6-1/2 ft. (2043mm),
2 ea. 4 ft. (1207mm)

8 carriage bolts: M8 x 100 with washers and nuts

Wood biscuits, glue, and screws

Spring mattress: 4 ft. wide (1200mm)

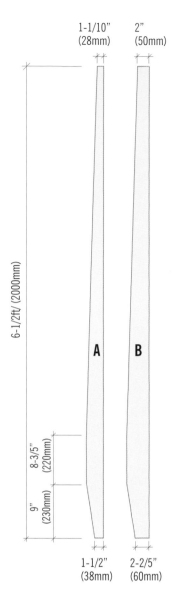

Instructions

1. Draw and cut pieces for the legs A and B.

2. Join the parts of the legs A and B with biscuits and glue.

3. Make 4 pieces 9" long (230mm) of the support leg C with the square wood (1-4/5" x 1-4/5" [45x45mm]) planed to triangular rails. Glue and screw them from the inside at the base of the legs.

4. Cut four 4" long (100mm) supports D (3/5" x 3/5" [16x16mm]) and bevel them on one end following the illustration. Glue them 1-3/10" (34mm) from the top edge of the legs.

5. Cut rails E and F (4/5" x 1-3/10" [22x34mm]) that will form the frame at the top. Cut halving joints in the ends.

6. Trim the glulam to the correct lengths for the sides of the bed G and H.

7. Trim the support boards I and J and blocks K (1-4/5" x 1-4/5" [45x45mm]) to correct lengths.

• Glue and screw the support boards I and J on the sides of the bed 4" (100mm) from the top edge of bed sides.

• Blocks K are glued in without screws on the long sides 4/5" (20mm) in from the ends and with their tops at the same height as the support boards I.

8. Assemble the bed and hold it together with clamps. It is important for the stability of the bed that the sides reach the ends in the corner on the legs.

9. Join rails E and F at the top. Bore through the rails and down in the support D and hammer in a nail to hold the rails in place.

10. Bore through legs A and B, side pieces G and H as well as blocks K and then join the bed with carriage bolts. Make sure that the holes are at different heights so that the bolts don't jam into each other in the blocks.

11. Number and mark all the parts before you take the bed apart so that you can assemble it the same way the next time. (If the holes do not meet at the exact same place in all the corners, it will be difficult to assemble the bed which can then be unstable.) You can mark the pieces by, for example, boring a little hole in an inconspicuous place on all the parts of one corner, two holes on all the parts of the next corner, etc.

12. Lay the spring mattress in the frame.

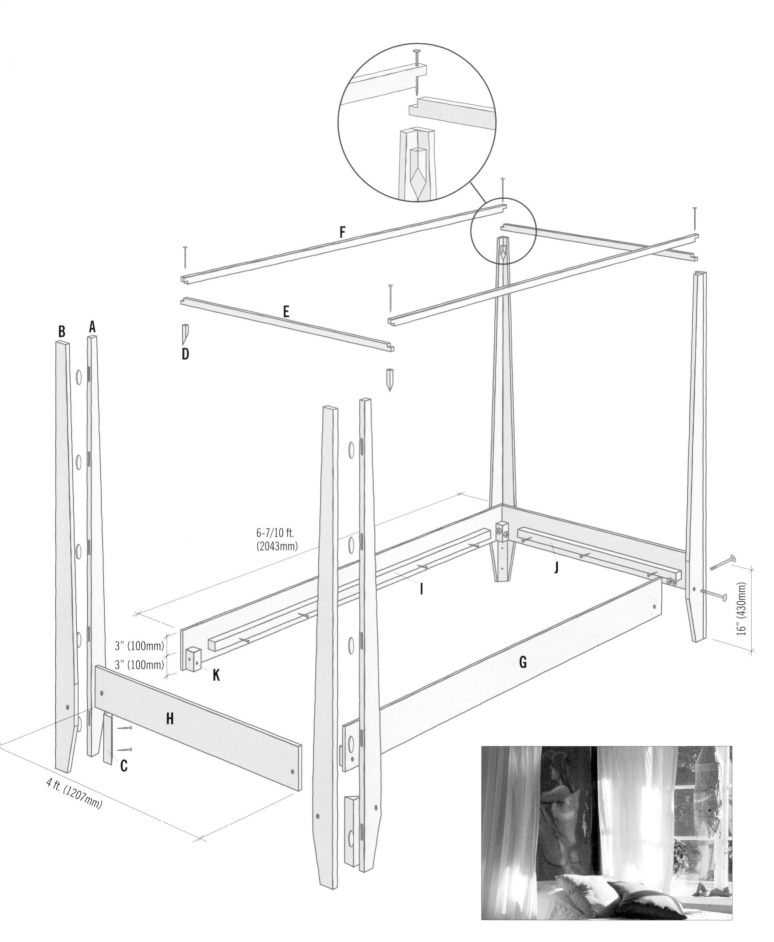

B A

F

E

D

6-7/10 ft.
(2043mm)

I

J

16" (430mm)

3" (100mm)
3" (100mm)

K

H

C

G

4 ft. (1207mm)

Inviting, soft, restful, and completely private are some of the feelings our guests have described when the curtains are drawn.

Night Table

Materials

Glulam sheet, 4/5" thick (20mm): 7-4/5" x 19-1/2" (200x500mm)

Plywood, 4/25" thick (4mm): 2-3/4" x 7-4/5" (70x200mm)

Wood biscuits

Glue

Screws

Instructions

1. Draw and cut the pieces from glulam sheet.

2. Assemble the pieces with biscuits and glue. Clamp and let dry.

3. Screw and glue the plywood pieces together.

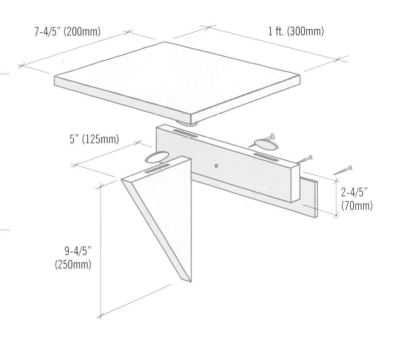

Playhouse

In our overgrown and wild garden, a little house is hidden in the middle of the yew and apple trees.

We had barely thought of it when the desire for a playhouse popped up, and we decided to build it in a somewhat hidden space. Of course, the day will come when the children are bigger and will be tired of having a playhouse on the lot. Our idea was that, according to necessity or opportunity, we could turn the little brown house with white trim into something more suitable. Perhaps a storage room, a small guest house, or why not a sauna? It remains to be seen.

Right now the cottage belongs to the children. Grandmother has been invited there many times for tea and cookies in the form of dirt balls with grass, water and one kind of insect or another. It is there that the children learned about cleaning with dish soap, plenty of water, buckets and rags. Everything in the house is thrown out onto the lawn. Plastic dishes are washed up and the floor scrubbed, sometimes with so much water that we have wondered why the floor tiles haven't just up and walked out.

I don't know who has had the most fun with the playhouse, the children when they play in it or Anders when he built it, although the children's pleasure has lasted longer. Anders thought it was fun as long as the building proceeded. Now he has to maintain the little house. And I think that he will soon suggest a new game for the children —painting the house themselves!

Playhouse

Materials

6 concrete blocks: 7-1/2" x 7-1/2" x 23" (190x190x590mm)

Insulation: 6 ft. (1.8m)

Dimensional lumber:

1-4/5" x 2-3/4", 15 yds. (45x70mm, 14m)

1-4/5" x 1-4/5", 39 yds. (45x45mm, 36m)

Unfinished tongue-and-groove board:

3/5" x 3-7/10", 120 yds. (17x95mm, 110m)

Decking, pressure-treated:

4/5" x 3-7/10", 11 yds. (22x95mm, 10m)

Stock panels:

1-1/10" x 4-4/5", 131 yds. (28x122mm, 120m)

Planed wood:

1-4/5" x 4/5", 16 yds. (45x22mm, 15m)

Cut wood:

¾" x 4", 33 yds. (19x100mm, 30m)

Triangular rails:

2" x 2", 6 yds. (50x50mm, 5.5m)

Roofing felt: 26 sq. ft. (8 square m)

Roofing glue

Nails and screws

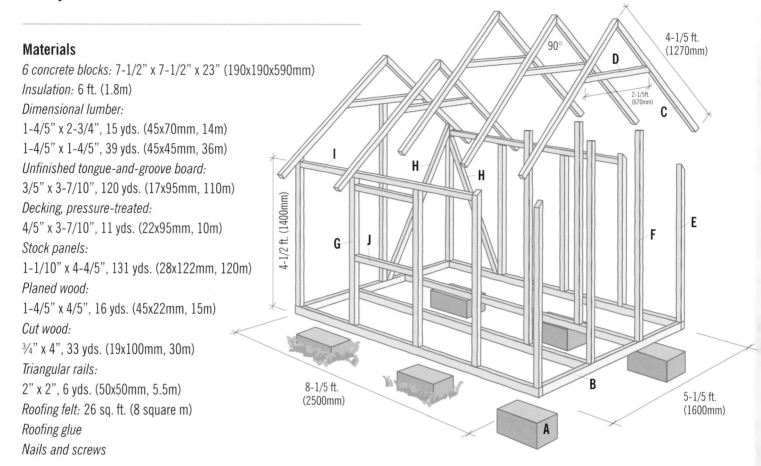

Instructions

1. Measure out the placement of the house and dig the holes for the concrete blocks A. Pour the aggregates and sand into the holes and arrange the blocks, each exactly level, in a rectangle that measures 8' x 5' (2500x1600mm).

• Measure the diagonal lines, which should be equal. Check with a level and straight board to insure that the blocks are all at the same level.

2. Cut the 6 pieces for the base frame B (1-4/5" x 2-3/4" [45x70mm]) and nail them together. Lay roofing underlayment between the concrete blocks and frame.

3. Cut pieces C and D for the roof beams (1-4/5" x 1-4/5" [45x45mm]). Miter cut parts C at a 45° angle on one end and on both ends of part D. Screw the parts together so all the roof trusses are exactly the same. Use the first one as the model.

4. Build the entire wall frame (1-4/5" x 1-4/5" [45x45mm]) on base frame B: uprights E, F, and G, oblique boards H, hammer bands I and noggins J for the window. Screw the parts together (it's easier than nailing them).

5. Put the roof trusses on. Be extra careful that the pieces are firmly and properly screwed together. Join them together provisionally with a couple of boards.

6. Lay the floor K with the tongue-and-groove panels with the smooth side up. Nail in the grooves or tongue so that the nail heads are not visible. Avoid splitting the boards.

7. Paint or glaze the stock panels L at least once before they are put into place. Nail on the panels, beginning at the lower edge with the groove downwards. On the gable points you can cut the panel boards roughly, nail them up and then cut following the roof trusses.

8. Nail the tongue-and-groove boards M on the roof beams. Cut off the tongue on the lowest part and begin from the bottom with the paneling upmost. Draw and cut off the ends when all the tongue-and-groove panels are in place.

9. Cut and screw on the triangular rails N along the cut edges on the short sides of the roof.

10. Roughly cut the roofing felt O into lengths. Begin from the bottom and fold the felt on the lowest section of the roof boards. Nail with roofing nails in the top edge and outwards to the lower edge on the underside of the roof.

Coat an approx. 6"-wide (150mm) strip of glue, out towards the roofing felt's top edge, lay on the next length, press over the glue and nail in the top edge. Continue the same way until the roof is completely covered.

11. Finish by gluing a narrow length over the ridge.

12. Screw the decking P firmly on the little terrace with rustproof screws.

13. Screw in the door and window frames. (See instructions for making the door and window on the following pages).

14. Paint all the frames Q, knot boards R, wind boards S and water boards T before they are cut and put into place. Use cut wood 3/4" x 4" (19x100mm). Measure, cut, and nail, but don't forget to paint, the end wood by hand. The knot boards should be cut at an angle on the lower edge so water will run off.

15. Install the little rails U (1-4/5" x 4/5" [45x22mm]) — don't forget to paint them first. Begin by attaching the crossbars with screws angled into the lumber of the house frame. Screw in the rails firmly from above first and then into the crossbars. These should be cut off at an angle at the lower ends.

16. Paint everything once more so that all the nail and screw heads are covered by paint.

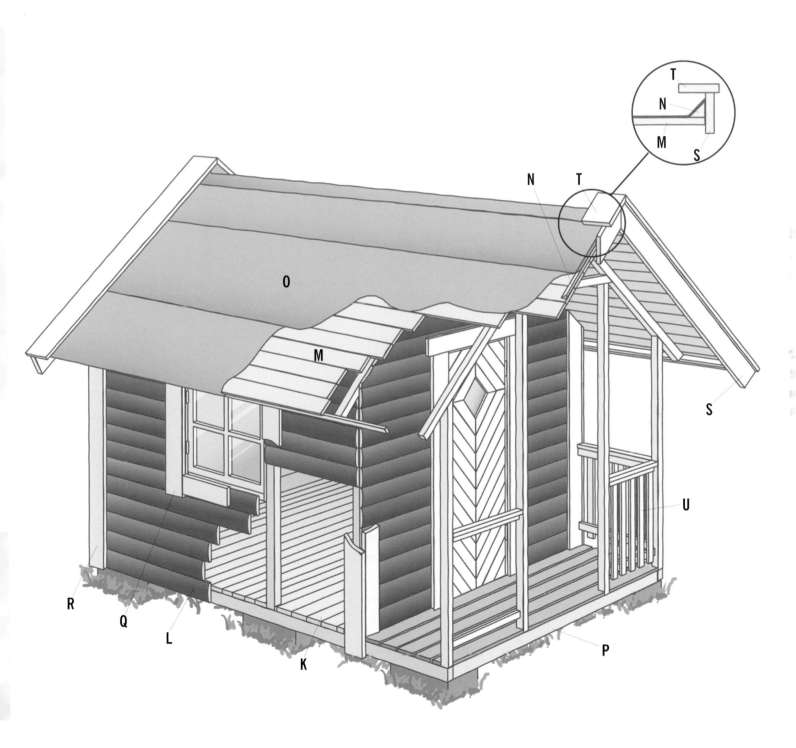

Window

Materials

Frame: Dimensional lumber, 1-4/5" x 2-3/4", 8 ft. (45x70mm, 2.4m)

Window sash: dimensional lumber 1-4/5" x 1-4/5", 8 ft. (45x45mm, 2.4m)

Muntins: planed wood, 4/5" x 4/5", 1 yd. (22x22mm, 1m)

4 pieces glass or plexiglass: 3/25" x 8" x 8" (3x205x205mm)

2 hinges

2 window hasps

Window putty

Wood glue, wood dowel pins, nails, and screws

Instructions

1. Cut a rabbet joint 1/2" x 4/5" (15x45mm) from the wood (1-4/5" x 2-3/4" [45x70mm]) for the frame A.

2. Cut the parts for the frame. Cut and chisel out the mortise and tenons for joining at the corners. Sand down the groove on the underside of the frame (between the side pieces) so that it leans slightly down and outwards.

3. Cut or chisel the recess for the hinges in the frame. Screw the hinges in securely.

4. Counterbore and screw the frame together.

5. Mount the frame aligned with the panel using long screws. Place small pieces of masonite in between if necessary. Use a level to insure that the frame is squared horizontally and vertically. Also measure the diagonal lines.

6. Cut a glass groove 3/10" x 2/5" (7x10mm) out of the wood (1-4/5" x 1-4/5" [45x45mm]) for the sash frame B.

7. Cut the parts for the sash frame. Cut and chisel out mortise and tenons for joining at the corners.

8. Cut a groove for the glass 3/10" x 2/5" (7x10mm) on two sides of the wood (4/5" x 4/5" [22x22mm]) for the muntins C. Cut the pieces for the muntins; cut and chisel out halving joints in the center and glue the parts together.

9. Bore the holes for the pins in the ends of the muntin crossing and in the frame of the window sash.

10. Assemble and glue the window sash frame and grid; clamp and let dry.

11. Cut or chisel out the recesses for the hinges on the frame of the window sash, checking the placement carefully. Screw the hinges in firmly. Hang the window and make sure it sits in a bit. Sand and adjust as necessary.

12. Apply two coats of primer on the frame and sash.

13. Set in the glass and secure with small tacks and putty.

14. Hang in the window sash and paint.

15. Attach the window hasp.

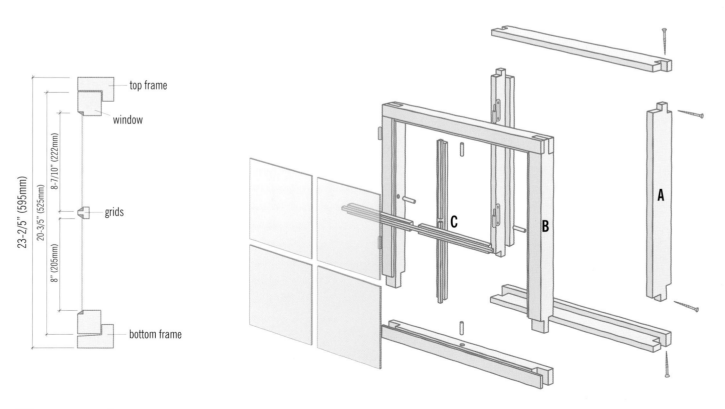

Door

Materials

Dimensional lumber:
1-4/5" x 2-3/4", 4 yds. (45x70mm, 3.6m)
1-1/10 x 2-3/4", 2 ft. (28x70mm, 600mm)
Building boards: 1" x 19-1/2" x 56" (28x495x1430mm)
Beadboard: 1/2" x 3-1/2", 11 yds. (12x92mm, 10m)
Glass rails: 1/2" x 9/10", 6-1/2 ft. (12x24mm, 2m)
Glass or Plexiglass: 3/25" x 8" x 8" (3x210x210mm)
2 door hinges
Door handle
Latex sealant
Nails, screws, and wood glue

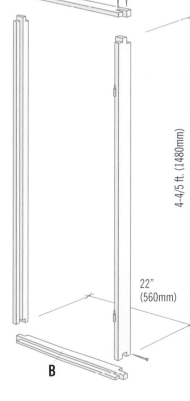

Instructions

1. Cut a rabbet and dado joint 1/2" x 1-1/2" (15x38mm) from the 1-4/5" x 2-3/4" (45x70mm) lumber for the doorframe A and from the 1" x 2-3/4" (28x70mm) wood for the threshold B.

2. Cut the pieces for the frame and threshold. Cut and chisel out the mortise and tenons for joining at the corners.

3. Cut or chisel out the recesses for the hinges in the frame and screw them in.

4. Counterbore and screw the frame and threshold together.

5. Mount the frame aligned with the panel using long screws. Place small pieces of masonite in between if necessary. Use a level to ensure that the frame and threshold are perfectly squared vertically and horizontally. Measure the diagonal lines also.

6. Mark the placement for the window on the building board C and cut it out with a jigsaw.

7. Draw a line at the center of the sheet from the top down where the beadboard D will intersect. Cut pieces of beadboard in the correct lengths and at a 45º angle. Glue and nail in the beadboard.

8. Cut and glue/nail the glass rails F on one side. Bead in a strip of latex sealant and set the glass in. Lay a strip of latex sealant along the edge of the other side of the glass and then glue-nail the glass rails there.

9. Cut or chisel out the recesses for the hinges on the door, making sure the placement is correct. Screw in the hinges securely. Hang the door and check to see if it needs to shift slightly. Sand and adjust as necessary.

10. Mount the door handle.

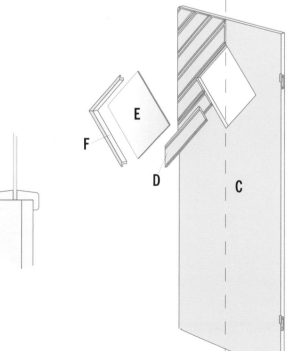

4-4/5 ft. (1480mm)

22" (560mm)

Schematics: Every square = 1cm (3/8 in).

☐ Candelabrum   ☐ Bookend   ☐ Children's bookend   ☐ Window shelf   ☐ Shelf over the Day Bed